The Ancient Schools of Wisdom

A Collection of Teachings from

Ramtha

Compiled by Diane Munoz-Smith

The Ancient Schools of Wisdom
© 1992 and 1996 Diane Munoz-Smith

All rights reserved. Printed in the United States of America. No part of this book may be reproduced or transmitted in any form or by any means without prior written consent of the Publisher, excepting brief quotes used in connection with reviews written specifically for inclusion in magazines or newspapers. This work is derived in part from Ramtha Dialogues®, a series of magnetic recordings authored by JZ Knight, with her permission. Ramtha® is a tradmark registered with the U.S. Patent and Trademark Office.

ISBN: 0-9652621-3-8

Published by:
Horus Publishing, Inc.
Suite 39, P.O. Box 7530
Yelm, WA 98597
Voice: (360) 458-1440
Fax: (360) 458-7816
email: goldenthr@yelmtel.com

Cover:
Photography: Mark Frey
Artwork: Ron Harvey

Books by Diane Munoz-Smith

"To Life! — A Collection of Prayers from Ramtha"

"Ancient Schools of Wisdom" also available in the German and Spanish languages.

ACKNOWLEDGMENTS

First of all, I would like to thank JZ Knight for allowing me to publish these teachings of Ramtha. From the time of their delivery in 1988 to this very day I am profoundly moved by the message they deliver. As I have had to pore over and over the words in the proofing and corrections, they have never failed to instruct me into a new area of understanding, so to be able to share these words with the world is an honor for me.

I would like to thank the following people for their love, confidence, expertise and support in producing the initial private publishing of *The Ancient School of Wisdom*: Diane D'Acuti of Ramtha Dialogues, my friends Rhiannon (Debi) Kerins, Cheri Wentworth, Gabriele Herpers, Mavis Cunning, Linda Furkay and my sons, David & Brien Munoz. Without their help this book could never have been published.

In this second edition of *The Ancient Schools of Wisdom,* I would like to extend my thanks and gratitude to Michelle Horkings of Horus Publishing, Inc., Greg Simmons of RSE Products and Services, and my friends, Kitty McKim, Kim Smith, Stephanie Millham and Caroline Couture. Thank you for all your help and assistance. And, also, I can't forget Pat Richker for her quality proofreading. Thank you, all of you!

And lastly, to Ramtha. Thank you for keeping your promise to return and for loving me into life.

THE ANCIENT SCHOOLS OF WISDOM

TABLE OF CONTENTS

INTRODUCTION 7
A SHORT HISTORY 8

THE NATURE OF REALITY
    Morning Session 13
    Afternoon Session 45

THE DESTRUCTION OF ANCIENT WISDOM AND ITS RESURRECTION
    Morning Session 69
    Afternoon Session 101

THE SEVENTH SEAL AND THE COMPLETED GARMENT OF LIGHT
    Morning Session 119
    Afternoon Session 149

OTHER RAMTHA TITLES 175

INTRODUCTION

The *Ancient Schools of Wisdom* was the last audience of its kind. Up to and including this teaching, all the attendants of Ramtha's audiences sat in chairs and listened to what he had to say. There was no hands-on experience, just information being delivered. It was called a "dialogue" but it was more like a soliloquy! For how could we understand without experiencing what it was he was talking about?

It seemed his plans were for the formation of a School of Enlightenment, where he could introduce disciplines and initiate us into experiences where we could experience the philosophy he gave to us and thereby have a truth to live by.

In the *Ancient Schools of Wisdom*, he delivered an overall summary of what we would have to learn. He discussed the nature of reality and how time works and how we have forgotten where we came from and why we were here. He tells us the history of how the ancient schools operated in times past and why their insruction was so precious: to awaken the forgotten God within. He explained that as the present civilization took hold, the ancient schools were obliterated along with everyone who attended them, except those who secreted themselves into the mountains and caves. The time had come to reinstate them in a new way. No longer were they to be hidden away and kept from the ordinary human being. He was designing a school that would be available to anyone who had the desire to know their heritage.

In this audience Ramtha also laid the foundation of the School of Enlightenment through seeds of information directed to the subconscious mind. The teachings he delivered would lie latent and sprout as the years went by and we contemplated, participated and grew in our spirituality. Over the following seven years and beyond, each sentence he delivered we would experience.

Directly after these audiences Ramtha changed his way of teaching us. As he explained in the audience, it was time for the "Teachings of No Words," and he wasted no time in initiating his students. The formation of his School of Enlightenment happened two weeks later at the Snow Mountain Park in Colorado. No more would we sit primly and properly around him just listening to what he had to say. With the School of Enlightenment he introduced the discipline of Consciousness and Energy (fondly referred to as C&E) and we were out of the chairs and fancy clothes and onto the floor donning sweat pants and other comfortable clothes, engaging the discipline of C&E, the hands-on experience of entering into the world of the void.

Since that time the school has grown and many more disciplines and teachings, including the sciences, have been delivered. Ramtha is a teacher of incredible depth and dimension. He never fails to instruct, entertain and deeply move his students with his knowledge and flair of delivery.

What I am presenting here in published form is the transcription of these audiences, held over a three-day period on May 13, 14, and 15, 1988. Since Ramtha has a unique way of speaking, using many unusual words and interesting grammatical statements, a few connecting words have been added here and there and the words have been rearranged in some places in order to maintain sentence integrity. However, for the most part, this is unedited and a true presentation of his teaching.

The tapes are available, as well as many other Ramtha books, tapes and videos. Please see the back of the book for a listing.

A SHORT HISTORY

JZ Knight had an extraordinary event happen to her one Sunday afternoon in 1977. Right in the middle of her kitchen appeared a glittering seven-foot being that only she could hear and see. He told her, quite simply, "Beloved woman, I have come to help you across the ditch." After the initial shock had subsided, the being, whose name was Ramtha, proceeded to explain to her who he was and what he was here to do.

> 35,000 years ago, Ramtha was a young boy living in Onai, a port city of Atlantis. As a Lemurian, he was forced to live in squalor and abject poverty, being treated worse than a common dog on the street.
>
> At the age of twelve he had the devastating experience of burying the last of his family, his mother and infant sister, who had starved to death as a result of the Atlatian laws. Embittered and filled with hate and anger, Ramtha set out to do battle with the unknown God of his people, the unknown God, whom he felt had deserted his family and his race. The only place he knew to do battle with this unknown God was to go to the highest mountain he could find, so he set out on the long journey with nothing but his hate to keep him going.

It took him two years to trek his way to the mountain and back. Once he arrived he cursed and threatened the God; there was no response. As Ramtha broke down and cried out to know why his people had been deserted by a God they revered, a beautiful woman appeared. She gave Ramtha a sword and told him to conquer himself.

Ramtha marched down from the mountain with a vengence, the huge sword given to him in tow and a terrible light in his eyes. When he arrived in Onai he stormed the gates and razed the city to the ground. The other Lemurians in Onai gathered around him and demanded that he bcome their leader. Together they formed the fiercest army that ever walked this plane and waged war against all tyrants. By the end of his lifetime, Ramtha's army had grown to two million strong and they had conquered two-thirds of the known world.

Ten years into his march, Ramtha and his army had won every battle they had engaged. Wherever he went, his terrible reputation preceded him; most believed the rumor that he was immortal. During this time the army had come upon a peaceful valley and decided to set up their encampment.

After they had been settled for three months or so, an emissary approached the encampment and requested Ramtha to meet with the council of the palace in the nearby city of Nabor. It was their hope that they could come to an agreement for a peace treaty. The Ram agreed to come to their city to negotiate.

Once in the palace and summoned to the council room, Ramtha was asked to leave his sword behind for this was a meeting of peace. Bowing to their request, he handed over his sword. Before he knew what was happening (but after he had the pleasure of insulting the council's arrogance), a man from behind ran him all the way through with a sword, which was then pulled out, leaving him to die.

Through sheer determination and will, Ramtha survived the attack. He was able to jam his fist into his gaping wound, stopping the flow of blood, and forced himself to stand up. His attackers were horrified! They were now sure that the rumors that he was immortal were true. They fled in fear. He sent a servant for his men, who gathered him up and took him back to his camp and placed him in the care of the legion of women.

For seven years Ramtha sat on a rock convalescing, suffering the degradation of being taken care of by women. His wound was so great and painful he could neither sleep nor move his body without assistance. With little strength left and being forced into solitude, he had nothing left to do but contemplate nature. Through this contemplation and examination of the life that teemed around him, the Ram came to understand who and what the Unknown God was.

When he finally came off the rock, he had reached such a state of enlightenment that he dedicated the rest of his lifetime to live what he had learned. In the sixty-third year of his march, Ramtha gathered his people around him, and for one hundred and twenty days he communed with them and taught them what he had learned. On his last morning the great Ram danced his ideal of the morning sun and, as it rose, he ascended, promising to return.

Ramtha's plan for his return to his people was to continue teaching them what he taught them so long ago. His plan meant that JZ (his daughter during his lifetime) would allow him to use her body to teach. The most important reason for this was to present a being that could not be seen and therefore not worshiped, for there was no form for the people to see. It would also demonstrate that God was neither male nor female and that God was the obvious unobvious, that which we could not limit to an identity.

And so in 1978, with JZ's agreement, Ramtha began holding Dialogues, teaching those who heard the call, his people of old. In 1988 he founded the School of Enlightenment, located on JZ's ranch in Yelm, WA, which continues this day.

— Diane Munoz-Smith
July 1996

*To all my fellow students in
"Ramtha's Little School of Enlightenment,"
that the value of what is contained
within these pages inspires, enhances
and encourages their journey,
as they have done mine.*

THE NATURE OF REALITY

MORNING SESSION

You are happy to be here? Yes? I am very pleased to be here this day in your time as you know it. And I am very pleased that you have paid homage to that which be I, for I accept always your love. So be it.

Let's have a drink and talk about what is real! Contemplate each word, that you embrace the word and allow it expand who you are.

From the Lord God of my Being,
To all that I am,
Unto the discovery of this journey
to know that which be I.
For the God that is within me,
I call forth
That the Imageless Being
Take over my life
And make my path
Straight.
Unto this day,
Come forth
And open my mind
And my book,

The Ancient Schools of Wisdom

> *That I may know,*
> *May be empowered*
> *To endure.*
> *So Be it.*
> *To the God within me.*

Always to the God within you. Let's get down to business.

I am very happy — that's your term — I am with great joy that you have made your pilgrimage here to learn this day. Well, not all of you that are gathered here are into learning. You're into wanting, not a lot of learning. Well, to those who hear this teaching this day, a reenactment of ancient knowledge, you're going to think this day. And your "buttons" are going to be pressed on the page you've been living on in the Book of Life that is your soul, your identity.

This teaching does not have to be long and drawn out; it doesn't need to be. But it's powerful. It will answer many, many questions as to why you have lacks, why you do not know, why you are helpless, what ignorance is and why you are powerless. It will answer many questions about your identity, the identity crisis, who are you.

But the knowledge is far greater than a magician's trick. Knowledge is far greater than ten thousand runners.* Knowledge is far greater than all the king's gold because knowledge, utilized and empowered properly, causes you to think and emotionally react. That begins to engage enlightenment as to the reality called self. It brings you closer to understanding the enigma that you are. And everything that is around you is a result of the enigma that you are!

Knowledge expands consciousness that never retards itself but goes forward. A hungry mind, a hungry soul. All of the adventures in life are a result of self and consciousness. They are energized through the ideal of what consciousness is — and self.

In my time I had done it all, having all the strokes a self could get! Strokes, that's your word; right? It really means the collapsing of the brain. But polish, perhaps, is a better word. But I would not have taken all of the king's gold and given up my knowledge because that leads to forever.

Truth is only truth when it is relevant to personal growth. And per-

---

* A runner is an experience that produces the opportunity to evolve. A runner can come in many forms: person, place, thing, situation, etc.

sonal growth is the reason that you are here. You are not here to be a king. And you're not here to be rich and you're not here to be poor and you're not here to be a victim/tyrant and you're not here to be a master.

You are here to consume the subconscious mind and make it conscious. You are here to awaken God. That is your journey. In the highway of light it is called forever. Never, ever shortchange yourself in giving up forever for a small desire. Never close off your mind to learn because you think you are incapable of learning or because your comfort zone demands you no longer have to think. Your beingness is the journey of evolution.

You shouldn't be here because you're afraid of changes.* You shouldn't be here because you're afraid you're going to lose your money or try to make more! You should be here for the Lord God of your being and the next moment to evolve to know that imageless being that is the power and the authority and the foreverness of all that is!

Knowledge; I have been a teacher of knowledge. And all the magic tricks were not a side show but only instruments in helping to bring that knowledge home in a form called "reality," because I already know where you are and where is the next step that turns those pages to the end, to the seventh seal. I am already at the seventh seal beckoning you through the channel on your path, laying down the footprints of tomorrow very evenly that you can walk in them all the way home! And it's knowledge that lays those imprints down; nothing else!

So now the teaching this day is to reenact an ancient cosmology, to reenact that which is termed an ancient wisdom that was taught in schools. "School" is your word but it was also meant there, because school meant "learning of I am," to reenact that. Certainly the place has changed and the school looks a lot different and you haven't been living here for a year.

And in these schools the first year you had to live through the testament of learning the knowledge of what the nature of reality was, and it took a year to learn that. And there were seven years in this school, with each year dedicated to the next step in evolution, the next dimension, the next consciousness, unifying all of them until you got to the seventh year. So in one day I am going to give you the teachings of the first year of the ancient schools.

---

* "Changes" refers to Ramtha's teaching given in May 1988 regarding the prophesies of the coming earth changes and how to prepare for them.

The Ancient Schools of Wisdom

Now the wonder of living one year of school. The calendar year has changed from ancient times. You are living on the Julian calendar. Those times were more adept to the Gregorian calendar in cosmology because part of the time there was no rotation of the sun; it was seen through a cloud cover. So a year is a little different than what we are speaking of today.

So what can we accomplish in a few hours? And how is the mind that can put that together in one day? Well, it's called "Ramtha."

You're going to miss a lot by not living this truth daily because, had you been living this truth in the ancient schools, you would have been in this presence every day and the energy would have built. In one year you'd have been an entity of fire.

So all I can do is to teach in words what this is and empower my word that it do something to you for a year. Now here is the complexity of the thing: We're going to do another year tomorrow! And I will say to them that what you will learn here this day, though in words, will press you in knowledge relentlessly to stretch that consciousness to understand the reality of the day before, to where you are opening up that brain and it is becoming activated through the pituitary.

Now here is the dilemma: because tomorrow I will say to them that this will last a year and they're going to come back the next day, and the next day is the evolution of the two days prior that has culminated six years of learning! Do you understand?

So Ramtha coming here and magically engaging you in knowledge about the nature of reality and the ancient wisdoms and the seventh seal is a lot to ask! Though it's not impossible; I can do it! But can you do it? And are you willing to do it? And to learn?

Now in one year, because that's what it will take and it will not be your year but a year that ancient wisdom was set into rotation, you will have learned in this audience all of its runners and the engaging of consciousness and miracles and the seventh seal. And the working of that year on top of this day will burn this mind open. So be it. The most arduous thing here is to break through your reality.

*N*ow the nature of reality.
What do you want? Tell me! *Ascension.*
What do you want? *Everything.*
What do you want? *Clarity.*

The Nature of Reality — Morning Session

What do you want? Speak up! *Knowingness.*
What do you want? *I want to become the Christ I know I can be.*
What do you want? *I want to become all that I can be in this lifetime and experience it all.* Give me five!
What do you want? *I want all that I am.*
What do you want? *To know.* To know what? *To know everything there is to know.*
What do you want? *I want knowledge.*
What do you want? *I want to be happy.* Happiness. *All that happiness is to me.* Happiness. But you see, all that happiness is to you is only the reality you can perceive happiness in.
What do you want? *I want to become and to know myself.*
What do you want? *Full consciousness into eternity.* Can't go to eternity without it!
What do you want? *I really want to understand and be and have superconsciousness, Ramtha. I really do want to get there and break through social consciousness.*
What do you want? *Joy.* Joy!
What do you want? *To learn everything I can.* To learn everything you can. Everything? No matter what?
What do you want? *To be all that I can be.* And you'll live long enough to know it, too.
What do you want? *To know that I'm God.*
What do you want? *To return to the Is in the whole nature of my beingness.*
What do you want? *I want to know and I want to live it.*
What do you want? *I don't know! Each time I think I know, it's not it!*
What do you want? *I want to know the totality of the God I am and to love it completely.*
What do you want? *Understanding.* Understanding? Of what? *Reality.*
What do you want? *To go home.* That's all?
What do you want? *Joy!*
What do you want? *Joy, peace, and sovereignty.*
What do you want? *To be the God that I am.*
Master, what do you want? *Wisdom and happiness.*
What do you want? *Joy and wisdom.*
What do you want? *To be all that I can be.*
What do you want? *I want knowledge and to go home.*

The Ancient Schools of Wisdom

What do you want? *To know that I am God in my being.*
What do you want? *I want to have fun!*
What do you want? *To grow spiritually and to appreciate who I am.*
And you? *To be.* To be? To be what? *All that there is, all that I am; to recognize it, live it.*

What do you want? *Joy.*

What do you want? *Knowledge and happiness.* Knowledge and happiness. What if you got knowledge and unhappiness? *I don't know!* What if wisdom made you sad?

What do you want? *I want fulfillment and ascension.* Fulfillment and ascension? *And ultimately ascension.*

What do you want? *To become all that I can become and to know the God inside me and knowledge.*

What do you want? *Eternal light and love.* Eternal light and love? *Eternal light and love.* What if I told you you already had eternal light now? What would you want? *The veils off.* The veils off; ignorance.

What do you want? *To be God realized.*

What do you want? *I want to be focused in my now in joy.*

What do you want? *I want to be judgmentless and unlimited.*

What do you want? *To know.* To know. To know what? *It's never changed: All.* All? But what if I told you to know all also brings sadness? *I know that.* So what about wanting to know all and joy? *I know that, too.* So then what do you want? *To know all, the way I want to know it.*

What do you want? *I want to stop going around in circles and go home.* The record, eh?

What do you want? *To remove this hard shell and to expose this sweet, soft spirit that I am.* It's your illusion that you haven't!

What do you want? *Knowledge and wisdom, and to go home to the Father.* You must know that knowledge engages experience and brings wisdom. *Yes, I want it anyway.*

Master? *I want to wake up.* To wake up! Yes! Some say that the moment of death is the true awakening. Still want to wake up? *Yes.*

What do you want? *To know and to be.*

What do you want? *Knowledge so that the divine fire of the Father within me will come forward and burn through everything in my life and change my reality.*

What do you want? *To expand my reality for wisdom and clarity to see myself as I am, without my mask.*

The Nature of Reality — Morning Session

What do you want? *I want to know and feel my oneness with God.* The nature of reality is that which you are living and yet do not have. Truth is, what you want is not your reality. Now the reality is living the lack in need of the want and the want is not the reality. The reality is that you don't have what you want.

Now how do you change all of that? Consciousness and energy, do you know what that is? The two principles of the universe or of that which is termed cosmic life. Some of you know that. Let me reiterate: There are only two principles in the universe. The universe is not moral; it is amoral. It is not subjective; it is objective. And with that virgin territory comes only two principles that create the nature of reality. They are called consciousness and energy. Consciousness is that which you perceive; energy is the active ingredient to manifest it into life. And the two create reality.

All that you know — forget the good and bad — but all that you know, that you have experienced, that you have seen, that you understand, that is tangible you, that makes up the identity that you are, you have created in your life through consciously energizing them into an experience. You don't know any more than what you consciously have endeavored to create. Creation then follows moral, good and bad — and, of course, there's the subjective element. But there are only two principles, consciousness and energy, and they constitute God, or the forever I Am that is I Am. The great slumbering void is God.

Now consciousness and energy are that which is termed an empowered light force whose destiny in evolution was, through involution, to descend elevations and degrees and levels of vibration. Consciousness and energy began on the seventh level of thought, created and lowered itself seven vibratory levels to become a conscious being, that which you are. Reality, that which is cellular mass, is created from the conscious mind that is awakened, and you are the "awakened" that does the creating.

Your destiny, which is in your soul, is like a book. And the title of the book is called Evolution — to evolve through seven levels, to reverse the process of involution and raise the frequency from mass back to the thought consciously awakened. God is asleep! Gods are the awakened adventurers consuming the unknown sleeping God to awaken consciousness.

That is your journey. Your journey is not to be a hairdresser or a robes man. Your journey is not to be that which is termed a lover to a certain individual. Your journey is not to be a king. Your journey is not to be the servant! It is to explore consciousness and energy to create and expand reality! You are the lights floating on that which is termed, as it were indeed, a sea of darkness. And the darkness is the void of space. And the light is consuming the unknown mind and making conscious that which has been unknown. That is your destiny: To be God realized.

Now when you consciously create on this plane, you are allowing light propellant from thought to enter into this brain. That light propellant begins to take form and the form is stretching consciousness. When it is realized is when it becomes an emotional abstract creation, that then that creation is made manifest through seven levels of time, distance and space to become the reality, that you can engage it on a physical being, stretching further the nature of reality and owning it in your soul. And then you turn to the next page, all the way back home again.

Now reality; what is real? It is a matter of opinion. And it is your opinion what is real to you and unreal to someone else. What is unreal to someone else is only due to the lack of experience and stretching of consciousness.

Now think of this abstractly. Consciousness and energy is that which you stretch your consciousness by taking out of the unknown mind a thought and giving it life. The energy therefore creates in the image of that thought reality. Then you have experienced; then you know.

There is so much you don't know because your reality has become your identity. And the identity that you now have talks about right and wrong, and that is always an inhibitor to an adventurous consciousness. You have an identity that is riddled with the fear of failure and success. You have an identity now that you have to support. Forget the consciousness; you have to take care of the identity! So all of your energy goes into keeping the identity alive and well and making a good image for yourself!

There is so much you don't know!

Think of a midnight sky and see one solitary star hanging low in

THE NATURE OF REALITY — MORNING SESSION

the east. Think of it as you rising. That light has to light up the entire void. That light has to grow and grow and grow until there is no darkness, until there only is the light. Now the light represents your consciousness. And the darkness, the sky, space, the void, represents the unknown mind, the yet-to-experience adventure, the experience of life. And it is your duty to consume, stretch, grow onto this plane of thought and make it alive; that is your destiny. Now consciousness and energy create the nature of reality.

Your lives are a result of your doing. What is in your life is a result of your consciousness because your energy is the handmaiden to that consciousness. What you want lies abstractly in the void yet to be experienced. What you are in is what your reality is, and what you continue to experience over and over and over is recycled experience. Get it? Boring stuff.

Now I said to you, "What do you want?" You were telling me what you were not. You had no idea how to be that "what not," just that you weren't that. So who you really are is minus that want, which means that you are the opposite of that want.

Now what did you say in that statement? You solidified a lack because consciously whatsoever give you energy to in a statement, you are. Because your energy will manifest the continuation of that lack. It doesn't feel bad that it makes you not God! Energy is the handmaiden of consciousness! Consciousness is the determiner of your reality, the energy just makes it happen and keeps you in this bubble that is called your reality, that keeps everything secure in that bubble and makes sure that you don't stretch any further than the identity feels necessary.

Listen, say you want to be God? Be it. Don't want to be it; be it. Because when you are, you are. And every probability that is in that void of that unknown mind will come rushing to you like a river.

And don't say you're not happy. The reason you're not happy is because you expect not to be happy; don't you understand? You're creating it! You have an option. Sit there and be depressed or be happy. Which do you choose? "Well, I'm going to be depressed, because I deserve to be depressed, because nothing in my life tells me that I am worthy to have joy!"

What does it take? "Well, it takes having a lot of gold; knowing you make the right choices; making everyone around me happy; living up

THE ANCIENT SCHOOLS OF WISDOM

and being this certain person for everyone. I can't change; you must understand that! I can't be happy! I have to be supportive."

And I look at them and say, peel, peel, peel!* Consciousness and energy. Consciously you have chosen to be depressed.

So how do you become happy? Turn the coin over and be it. You don't have to have a reason to be happy. You just have to make the choice; that's all! Why must you have a reason? Isn't life reason enough?

Wake up! I'm driving something home that it took a year in the schools long ago for adepts to learn. Why couldn't they levitate? Because the force of gravity proved to them that they couldn't! And yet who created gravity? Who keeps it in place?

"I'm going to put it there and it's going to stay."

"I am going to do this in my life and that's how it's going to be and it's going to stay right there!"

"I'm going to marry this person and we're going to be happy!"

Yes? These are things you say!

"I am putting my crystal right there and it's going to energize whatever it's on."

Don't you understand? You force the issue of gravity! Don't you know in consciousness you reverse it? It takes a year to learn that in an old school.

I'm driving home a point to you in simple analogy of what I hear you say! And you wail and cry and bawl and moan and shake your fists and call to me and say you need help? The best help I could give you is to ignore you! Because what does it take to press you? Is your pain so intense that it will pull you through this tunnel? Must you get so depressed that one ray of sunshine alone can bring you absolute joy, instead of having someone make you happy?

Now you think about this. The nature of reality is created by your conscious thinking, and the energy to that conscious thinking creates that reality. And you live in this nice, tight, little bubble that doesn't go anywhere. Now that is the simple truth of the nature of reality.

Now what about all the window dressings? Right and wrong; the identity crisis that you have? Those are all subjective to civilization. When you get civilized is when you lose common sense. When you get

---

*Ramtha is referring to an older teaching in which he tells us we must peel ourselves like an onion.

The Nature of Reality — Morning Session

civilized is when you no longer think, you no longer reason and you no longer have the courage of ancient warriors to be the intrinsic, powerful entity that is behind this mask in every one of you. Because "civilized you" has to live within the abiding law and the morality of good and bad and the mistakes and paying for them. And you have set up all of this into a reality by consciously accepting it. Therefore when you engender to stretch, to experience what you have not experienced, you consciously have already set up the punishment because you have broken the law. And you're always going to get caught because there is no one pulling any strings in this bubble except you and how you think.

Now is that applicable for everything? Everything. Do you know why you stop growing and you're civilized? Because civilization says that it is the epitome of the civilized man. And its technologies are at the height of achievement. And its society bends to the Rule of One, or law, and you stop being you. And this crust begins to encase you, this altered-ego image begins to be you. And the beautiful, awesome entity, the imageless Lord God of your being, becomes a faint echo of yesterday. And it hides behind the curtains and supports the drama of the altered ego, who now is living in a right-and-wrong, civilized, high-tech world.

And God is "out there" and you struggle to bring it in here. You do everything in your reality to support the image. And the God inside allows it to go on because this has chosen. And you're stuck on page three in the Book of Life: power, pain and copulation. You struggle to find love and an identity.

It's on page four, but you can't turn the page because if you turn the page you'll shatter the identity! You're going to make people unhappy because you've become yourself! When they're miserable, you're feeling "up;" no one wants that! But you are doing what is right for you; you are living a truth that is correct for you.

And you're rattling everyone's bubbles, you see? Because you live surrounded by other little bubbles. And they're all the same size as you are because you can't have a bubble equal to you unless it is the reflection of what you are! And when you start growing, you shake all of the other bubbles — all of the other realities — up. And no one wants you to rock the boat; get it?

So what consciously happens to this power that created the universe? Where is the energy that set the sun into motion? It is plucking an eyebrow off of your face! And where be that which is termed the consciousness that made the trek of falling seven levels in vibration to engender mass?

This is the only plane with time, you see. This is the only plane that has the time-space matrix. It is the only plane with the spiral of time — matter/antimatter, that which is termed, as it were indeed, gravity/antigravity, blinking exactly opposite of one another. This is the only plane that has distance based on time.

The God who set the universes into motion is now into mass, equal to that which it created, making a journey in time. Time, everything here takes time. Consciously created, it takes time to manifest. It has to! That is the law of this level! It is the law! It is not the law on another level; it is only this level! So here you have these Gods with this great power that are now locked up into supporting an identity that will make everyone happy, and page four in the book never gets turned in this lifetime. Now you keep coming back here because in this Book of Life it says you will create reality until you have owned seven levels in mass, seven pages of conscious reality.

Now in your reality, on page three, it is very limited. It has to be because you have to abide by the rules.

So you say to me, "I want this; I want to know the God that I am; I want to be all I can be; I want to ascend." My God, you haven't even lived! "I want to be happy; I want to have peace; I want to have wisdom."

Don't you know you have to expand your consciousness in order to gain wisdom because you've got to create the ideal of that consciousness in order to experience it; then you have wisdom? Don't you know joy is a choice? It comes from making a choice to continue to roll, to evolve.

The unhappy souls are those who do not evolve. They are the ones who live in pain and misery because they do not change. It is vital. It is the essence. Don't you know evolution means change? But you keep yourself from doing it because you have fear in your reality and that fear keeps you going only so far. So simple is this understanding that you will intellectualize it and make it so complicated. You will not understand it because it's your excuse not to grow because of fear.

Think about it. The sun is only up when you see it. Close your eyes and it doesn't exist. It only takes a moment to be happy; there's a lot to be happy about. It only takes a moment to stretch this consciousness to say, "What's next?" It only takes a moment to go right through all of the civilized thinking to the abstract thought that is waiting in the unknown mind.

All of you think your subconscious mind sits here (the neocortex); correct? This is conscious right-and-left stuff. Somewhere in between is the key to enlightenment. Right behind the ear is the brain that can perceive other dimensions; there is a little part of your brain that can do that. Well, it's "dead." Nothing is working in it!

And somehow you have this feeling that close to the pineal is where the subconscious mind lurks. And if you can only take enough drugs or get drunk enough — if that's your excuse — or meditate enough or do enough, you can open all of this subconscious stuff up! Well, you see, subconscious mind isn't locked into your brain; it's everything you are! It's everything that's around you. It's the furthest star that's in front of you. It is all around you; it is permeating that which you are! Because it's the glue that keeps you held together in this understanding. Subconscious mind is not who you were in your past lifetime; that's on page two. It has nothing to do with subconscious mind. You can't remember who you are because you learned what it was you were supposed to be!

Subconscious mind is yet to be explored. It is the great abstract; it is the great probability and possibilities of all that awaits you every moment of this existence. It is there where genius lies, where remarkable thoughts lie. It is there where opportunity is waiting to be cut out of the void and made into the pattern of life. And all you have to do is turn your head forward and understand. "Consciously, if I engage the subconscious mind, it will come to me." Yes, it does. Listen to me! The nature of reality, your world, reflects who you are, what you think, what you feel. Your world reflects only that which you have created. It doesn't reflect what you have not created; only what you've created, who you are.

If you are a victim, you are a victim of your own creation because it hasn't occurred to you that the same consciousness that created the experience has to evolve to a higher consciousness in order to absolve the experience as wisdom, instead of making it a problem! You have to grow! The same consciousness that creates a kingdom cannot be the same consciousness that will evolve it. It takes a higher consciousness to evolve the kingdom; not the same one you created it with!

The Ancient Schools of Wisdom

Reality. Think about it. Everyone in your life is a reflection of who you are! They can't be in your life unless they represent a facet of your consciousness! You identify you through all of the people in your life! That's how you see yourself. That's why you need them, to piece together the mystery of I Am. And they're reflecting to you equal to what you are.

Now who created them there? Like draws like. Opposites do not attract; like attracts in consciousness and energy. You can't consciously create and then have the energy bring forth the opposite because you didn't create the opposite; you created the ideal! Do you understand? Wake up! Do you understand?

Now the first set of runners is everyone in your life that makes up and constitutes the nature of your reality, every single one of them. I want them to come back to you and I want you to see the facets of who you are. And the moment you do that, you will evolve your reality greater. Because it will take a higher consciousness to see yourself in them than the consciousness that brought them there in the first place. Bargain? So be it. Now they're all the same size as your bubble. There's no king bubble; there's no queen bubble and then smaller bubble servants. There are only consciousness and energy realities glued to one another who represent each other and the same reality.

Don't you know why you do not have a physicist in your life? What would you do with them? What would you talk about over lunch? What would you discuss after-hours? Could you relate to that person? The greater question is could they come down and relate to you? Why don't you have a physicist in your life? Because that which is termed, as it were indeed, mathematical understanding and solving the problem of the universe just isn't your bag in that direction! That's why they're not a part of your life. So why is the person that you call a jerk in your life? Because you're a jerk. Get it?

Conscious creation: Energy comes right out here; energy creates the idea; you experience the idea; that stretches your consciousness to make a higher consciousness that will take an emotional experience and write it in the Book of Life. And that experience constitutes a facet of who you are. Every person you have experienced is sitting there in your reality and they are a reflection of who you are.

Want to get rid of them? "Some. Well, a few. I don't know, maybe all of them!" The moment that you look at them you will see what they

The Nature of Reality — Morning Session

are telling you about you because you never see them; you only see you. When they tell you that they want something, you go along with the want because that's what you want. So what they're really saying is, "You want this, so I am doing it." And you give them permission.

If they do something you don't want, there is friction in your reality. You cannot relate to them. "Well, I don't understand you at all! Why are you doing this to me? Why are you doing this? You know this doesn't make any sense at all! You know that makes me unhappy."

"Yes, that's why I'm doing it!" Do you understand? You never see them. On a conscious level you only see self.

But when you begin to look at them and say, "What are you to me?" it will stretch your consciousness because many people stay in your life because you have not resolved the wisdom of their experience. "Who am I to you? And who are you to me?" When you see what you have gained from it, it will take a high consciousness, which means it has already stretched and expanded. The wisdom is now realized, the light goes on and the reality gets bigger. And unless they're growing too, they give you up. The nature of reality.

Now there's not one of you in this audience that can sit here and say, "That is a wonderful teaching but that doesn't apply to me because nothing in my life makes sense." You don't make sense so nothing in your life will make sense; don't you understand? If you're out of control so is your life. Get it? And if you're living in fear, the "boogyman" is behind every corner. Get it? If you're unhappy, everything's going wrong in your life; get it? If you're in love, everything is spring; understand? Get it?

Isn't it amazing, entities, how you can be so miserable and Mr. or Mrs. Wonderful walks into your life and it's just as if yesterday never existed! You're so happy and lighthearted and you own the world and you're generous and kind and smiling, instead of being a wretch? And it only takes a wonderful reflection of yourself to do that.

And Mr. and Mrs. Wonderful are wonderful only because they reveal something beautiful about you! That's the only reason you love them! Someone comes along and mirrors to you the possibilities of what you are. Well, it is enough to make you want to sing a song, chase butterflies through the meadows; you know? Do you understand? And that passion and that heat that is running through your body is only a joy about the possibilities of who you are. Haven't you ever heard that term? "I just can't believe you love me. You're so wonderful, so beautiful, you're so rich, you're so poor. You're just what I was looking for. But I cannot believe you would like me!" What an arrogant statement! Of course they like you! You created them there! Get it? Because there was nothing in your life that was mirroring or stroking you, so it was time for a change. And you got all happy and your cheeks looked wonderful — someone had been pinching them — because you got to experience a probability about who you are. Self; this is the journey of self.

Now that is how reality works. Don't you know you're poor because you think that's all you deserve? Do you know how many lifetimes you've gone through guilt and being conditioned in your soul to feel guilty? Do you know how many generations that you have been conditioned on page three in your book to think little about yourself, that you are a sinner, that you are born in corruption? With God somewhere "out there" you are hoping you're going to do good. You can't even begin to do good; you don't even know what it is! You just can't help doing all those things that you do. And someone tells you you better repent and your soul is crying out, "For God's sakes! We needed to do this! Wake up! I had to do this to understand this. Why should I repent? I gained wisdom."

And someone says, "Shut up! That's the devil talking! Shut up!" And the God of your Being says, "How dare you say that to me!" And so it keeps nagging at you, "You've got to do this! You've got to feel good about yourself! God isn't out there, stupid! It's me talking to you! Listen to me! Yes!" That is what it is saying! It's your consciousness in here saying, "Read the bottom of the page, please! Reason, for God's sake, for my sake, so that we can get through this ordeal!"

Well, you've been conditioned not to hear yourself because it's supposed to be the devil or something evil or the dark forces talking to you! Don't you know it's your God talking to you? It's saying, "If you don't do this in this lifetime, we're coming back in the next lifetime and you're going to do it!" Yes! It also says to you, "Listen stupid, the only way we gain wisdom is to experience this thing. Then you know you never have to do it again. Then you can go on to something else! And I'm not going to leave you alone until you do this because we have to turn the page! We've got to get on with this business. It will give you up! Trust me, trust me, trust me!" Does that sound familiar? Yes? Ah! Praise God! It is talking to you! Yes!

Now what is the sweet, imageless, wonderful personality that's inside of you doing? Well, it's a grand character: It's full of boisterousness; it is full of daring adventure; it is a romantic; it loves life; it swoons over a blue moon! It finds joy in raindrops! And animals find peace there with this entity because there is no anger, there's no violence, there is no hatred, there is no bitterness, there is no sorrow. There is only pure love coming from this imageless being that's sitting in there telling you, "Listen. I'm really you! Get rid of this superficial person. It's me. I am the Lord God of your being. We are creating your reality not to show you what you look like, but what you're made of! Time is running out! We've got to turn this page! There is more for you to experience! We have to experience this! You have to awaken. Remove it and let me come out! Trust me. I will take you down no path that will destroy you, for I am forever." So be it.

Well, reality is this expanding, unseen, beautiful entity that all of you are. The teaching "Behold God" and for me to look upon all of your faces was not to see your face, but to see that which is behind the face, the light, the consciousness, the empowered energy! Behold that which creates divinity! Man and woman are not made divine! They create it to behold God. To see the second coming of Christ is not to look in the sky but to look upon "behold the holy" that sits in this audience! To that God within that says, "Keep it up, Ram, keep it up! Keep it up! Yes!"

That is what I address and it is that that I speak to. It is that that hears my voice and responds because it knows, and I am looking at it and not at you. For I love not the identity but the imageless being that is empowered, that I know can hurl a universe into being, that is stuck in a reality created by the image and thinks that its self worth is based on that which it's created in its imageless being — all to pacify the image!

Consciousness and energy, simple stuff! What you think, you are! What you credit yourself is your kingdom. If you see the image, you deny the God. And if you do not evolve because you have excuses, you have created them in consciousness, manifested them in energy to be your blocks. No one blocks your path to awaken. Don't you know what the term "awaken" means? Get with it! "Awaken" means when this comes out, this is Christ realized, God-man-woman realized! That's what it is; that's what the Ram became, a powerful light. It was not the Ram but the unknown God. It was unknown because I had not looked in here!

You are so powerful you create your lack and, through conditioning, you create your unworthiness. The God within you would never say it is unworthy because it knows that it is the worth of all things. It is the life force, the principal cause; it would never say that. Only the image says that.

"I have done all of these things in my life. God, have I made mistakes! And they haunt me!" They haunt you because you have not seen them as wisdom instead of mistakes! And they keep coming back, waiting. And that God within you says, "Come forth! Come forth!" It brings all of your misery up; don't you understand? The God within your being keeps your past in front of you, for you to say, "It is finished." To say, "I have gained wisdom from this that it may be written in my book, in my soul, called Life." Then it gives you up and then the sun begins to shine upon you! The light that is within you begins to come forth.

Your mistakes keep coming back because your God is bringing them back because how can wisdom be a mistake? But it takes wisdom to evolve! And every step of evolution peels away the image!

Listen to me! Listen. This lifetime is just another character; this is another character. This whole lifetime represents a day in eternity. It's another character that you have created for the sole purpose to experience, through the character, to turn the pages. The character is not you! It's you that's creating the character for the sole purpose of an experience, maybe one small experience.

Where is the audacity that a child can come into a family and live to be only twelve days old and then perishes? It came back for one experience; that was enough. Or why is it a kind person that perishes, for seemingly they are the ones who die young? Where are the great people who bring peace and truth and light? Why must they always have their flame extinguished? What in their reality has caused that? It is because their purpose has been accomplished because now that word will live on. That is enough; that is all they needed to turn the page. They are illuminated beings.

The character this lifetime is a crack in the light of all eternity; it is not you! It is a shell. It was created just to learn one thing, not so it would continue to live in that groove, not so it would continue to repeat over and over and over mundane experience. What does it take for you to know you own it? Are you repeating it for the sake of your

The Nature of Reality — Morning Session

image and your reality and everyone that is attached to your reality, that it gives credibility to the image?

Or are you doing it because in every swing in the spiral you are continuing to gain? In one lifetime, one, you can own in the space-time matrix every part of consciousness, in one lifetime, in the same character. But the character gets burned away on page four in the book. Are you listening? If your monkey-mind is going now, it's your image because it is threatened by what is within it.

Now pagan cosmology, pagan dogma and worship, is set on an individual personality, that that person has that lot from the beginning of their life to the end of their life; they are born under a sign or a planet. That is complete reversal of power. The truth is when people speak that way, they are completely ignorant of their divinity, that it is their evolution that will create for them. And they are completely ignorant as to the power of the mind given free rein and what it can create in reality, because dogmas and religions are based on the image and not what is within. Because what is within has its allegiance to the all-in-all — that which it is — the essence that you are.

This wondrous being, this light, it will tell you when it's over. It will tell you when it's finished. It is charitable. It is the essence of grace. It is unconditional love. It is jolly laughter. It is life.

This entity inside of you, to what I say "Behold God," doesn't live by any laws except that it is a lover of life, the life force. It knows when the experience is over and it tells you so. It's the image that holds onto the experience, that causes the pain and the sorrow and the problems and makes up all of the excuses and denies itself. The image never wants to let go of what made it an image. The God inside says, "We have to release this." This voice will keep telling you that.

This imageless being can create a reality that is astounding and, every step of the way of stretching consciousness and manifesting that consciousness, brings you closer to the light within you. It takes away the clouds and it dissolves and burns away the image.

The nature of reality is to be illuminated. It only takes a moment to be illuminated. And then in the next moment, once it's experienced, it's yesterday's news! And then there's the next moment of illumination. You say that this life is so hard. It's so hard because you make it so hard.

This unknown stretches forever. In the unknown lies all of that which is termed the human potential, probabilities, genius, options. It

THE ANCIENT SCHOOLS OF WISDOM

awaits for you to consume it, to have one abstract thought, to be able to hold onto that thought and move with it. Not everything you do should be because of the "bottom line" as it is termed. Not every thought should be suckled around money. A great thought can be that which illuminates and burns, in a moment, away the image!

Now the nature of reality. There was a grand, grand, handsome man, young, virile, impassioned, sizzling, hot! He came from a very wealthy family. He strolled around in the finest of silks and velvets and cloth of gold and silver. And he rode a steed as white as snow, and the horse had no dirt upon its personage. They lived in the finest part of town, the only two-story home in the village. That way they were one up above everyone else!

Now there came a conflict of revolution. And this entity, who had lots of friends and lots of women, of course, tattering after his heels, was called to go and fight for the village. After all, it would give the family quite an esteem to have a son who was a hero on top of everything else. So he was piled into his mail and armor and set upon his horse. And with great fanfare he and his friends galloped down into a saffron sun. And his parents would not hear from him in quite a while.

Now their reality, you understand, was the best of everything, and they lived their image through their young and virile son. Well, needless to say, everything was "copacetic." The mother and father had nothing going on in bed but on the surface everything looked wonderful, except they lived everything through their son.

Now on the battlefield, needless to say, on the first charge Prince Charming got knocked off his steed. And the heavy mail which he was wearing got hung up in that which is termed the metal stirrup, and the horse dragged him quite a distance.

And as the horse stopped nearby at a small pond, it began to graze. And the young man lay on his back and looked up at the stars. A black night it was, not a moon in the sky. And at that moment the whole of the unknown opened to this entity because for a moment he wasn't the image. Nothing that was familiar was around him; he was on his back and helpless. And in that moment he looked at the great void and understood reality, understood God, in a moment. He had a revelation. The entity at the moment of that revelation lost consciousness, and thus began a fever and a sickness that would purge and test his life for weeks.

THE NATURE OF REALITY — MORNING SESSION

And his mother and father sat at the end of his bed praying, crying and weeping, watching their son go through deliriums. He would scream and holler and curse. At one point he spat; it landed upon his body. He teetered on the "edge."

And then one fine morning — oh, yes it was! — a sparrow in flight landed upon this entity's window and it began to sing a melody. Ah, the melody of life! A haunting, joyous symphony calling him forth, "Come." He awakened to the melody and went to find the bird. The bird led him out onto the roof top and then began to fly and say, "Come with me. Come. You can do it!" Needless to say, they thought he had lost his mind.

Now this entity, after the day of awakening, never was the same and spent many hours in the fields of scarlet poppy. And he looked upon the stone and contemplated the energy and the magnificence of the stone. And once he experienced a great and beautiful butterfly and watched its delicate limbs and the hovering of oriental fans as it breathed. And the entity contemplated a blue sky and remembered a black one.

It could never be. And when they lay upon him silks and scarlet cloth, he tore them off. He did not want them. And they put before him a feast for a king; he ate simply. And instead of hanging out in the tavern — the Prancin' Pony no less — and sharing a brew and stories of glory mostly untrue, he was found under a great oak contemplating what he thought he knew.

This entity finally one day, from the meeting of a great man of God who was a hypocrite, tore off all of his clothes and wandered into the wilderness, never to return to the house of his parents. And he stripped down his clothes not because he was an exhibitionist but because the clothes were the last burning away of the image of this man. And he walked naked into his life, into the wilderness, and there he had a closeness with all things that were living. A wild animal would sit at his feet, and he would find joy sitting amidst birds of silver wings.

The entity struggled to make a monument, not of gold or silver, but of the humble earth, of manure and clay and straw. And it was to stand for the glory of what he saw in the sky that night in an abstract thought. And the entity lived the purest form without the image and became all that life was. He had burned away the image that he came in with, to learn from in one lifetime, to burn it away to allow the light to emanate from within him to be the glory of God, God-man realized. And at the end of his life, after having been ostracized by the very thing that he loved, he became Christ. And his name was St. Francis of Assisi.

Now what has he to do with your reality? He had a moment and a revelation when he understood. And in the next he made the choice to burn away, to know.

You ask me to know! You want to know! What do you think knowing is about? It is to burn away the excuses, to experience, that you may know. The entity burned away his reality to be who he was, that which was imageless within him. Did someone choose him? Did God from afar or an angel or a UFO choose him to be who he was? Was there something special about him that you don't have? No! Just a choice. Cutting away all the fat and saying consciously, "This is what I want because what I want is what I lack, and I must fill the lack in order to know. And in order to know, I will be all that I can be."

No, he was no different. He didn't come into that life to be St. Francis, and he abhors the word "saint." He came into life to fulfill the character that had everything; he couldn't ask for anything more! Except maybe a credit card. Thank goodness he didn't have those!

But you see, you have more in technology than he did in his time. You have captured electricity in a ball of light, and he had a beeswax candle. But it doesn't make any difference what your technology is; it is the same energy. And in his lifetime he came through to own, and in a moment had a choice to change, and he elected to do so. And the change took him to the other side of his experience, naked in the power of what was within him, because nothing on him disallowed the love to flow out. Nothing that he wore disallowed the beauty to come forward. There were no jewels on him to say that he had grace. He just was. All of the attributes change.

Now you have no excuse, none of you. Is there a saint in you? You bet there is a saint in you! Will the world recognize it? Probably not, and you're better off if they don't! Is there a kindred spirit who is fearless in you? Yes, the God within you doesn't know any fear because there is nothing to fear; it is life itself. It realizes that everything that you're engaged in as the image is merely an illusion that you keep thinking you have to have!

And don't be generous and regret it. Don't give grace and hate yourself for it! Don't pretend you love — you liar — when you don't! The image can never do that! God within does it; it is it! It is the epitome

THE NATURE OF REALITY — MORNING SESSION

of grace and giving and love and power. That is the illuminant.

What is the nature of reality in regards to that? The illuminant is on page four. That begins the burning away of the image, of the thing you think you are. Listen! If you think you are something, then you are! If you think you cannot live without something, then you cannot! If you think you are without, you are without. And if you base all of this knowledge on the stock market, you are a loser anyway because you'll never get out of that groove until you realize that is an illusion. Death is the moment of awakening because in death the image dies! There's nothing but a corpse laying there pumped full of preservatives. For what, by God? You're going to come back and pick it up?

You were the essence that gave it virility and life and magnetism and power. It wasn't those eyes and their color that made them sparkle! It was that brilliance behind those eyes. It wasn't those hands that held softness and tenderness. It was the charity in the soul of the entity that never dies. You're just on to, perhaps, page four.

New character. You plot out what life you're going to come back into — hopefully you can come back — what gene pool you're going to choose from, what you hope to look like because you need to still look like that because that works into the plan, because everything you do has got to center around a sandbox. And some need large sandboxes and others only need a small one. But it all has to work in order to achieve the option to engage another friction in the time-space matrix in order to make it happen!

You won't remember who your body was in the last lifetime; who cares? Dead meat! It's who you are now. It's that power, that vitality, that consciousness power, that energy. And what kind of reality can they choose? Expand it. Move it. Call it forth. Stop saying, "I want," and say "I am." Start calling forth the Lord God of your being when you need something. Be it. Stop looking at your life and complaining and bitching about it! If you're a bitcher and you're unhappy, it's time you get off your rump and change your consciousness, attitude. Then the energy will change the reality.

Stop complaining. Are you waiting for all the catastrophes to happen to prove you did something right? Where is that coming from? The world has to die and prove you did right in this lifetime? Come on. Knowledge was there so that you could live through it, to make decisions to continue to expand. It is only a part of the process! It is not the prize!

The Ancient Schools of Wisdom

Now reality. You're a victim; you made yourself one. If you lack, then your whole life is based on lack. You must cease in thinking you're going to move by staying in this groove; it's not going to happen. Because all you do is just dig deeper in the groove. Nothing happens in your life. Nothing begins to make things go.

Now there are two principles. What are they? *(Consciousness and energy.)* What do they do? *(Create your reality.)* Whose? *(Mine.)* So what do you think of yourself, consciously speaking, of course?

Now the same God that Francis is, the same stuff — proper term? There are better terms but "stuff" is all right — that he is made out of, so are you. The same stuff Yeshua ben Joseph is made out of, so are you. The same stuff Buddha Amin was made out of, so are you. And the same stuff as Kubla Khan was made out of, so are you. And the same stuff that Genghis was made out of, so are you. And the same stuff that Nero was made out of, so are you. And the same stuff that Justinian I was made out of, so are you. And the same stuff that Newton was made out of, so are you. And the same stuff that Elizabeth I was made out of, so are you. And the same stuff as the jester in the court of Henry III, so are you. And the same stuff that Hitler was made out of, so are you. And the same stuff God is made out of, so are you.

Now I rain on your parade of excuses because you create excuses and you give them power. You create the blocks so nicely because you refuse to think any further. You've got your little ribbon of how you think. You've got your little slogans that you say every day, that don't mean a hill of potatoes, beans or oats. You've got your little dogma that you practice every single day. It makes you feel good about yourself. That isn't the stuff I'm talking about!

There's no reason not to move forward except that you're afraid. And being afraid, fear, comes from the image, the altered ego because the altered ego is comprised of the first three pages of the Book of Life, copulation, pain and power. That's what its identity is made out of. Don't you understand? Fear is the guardian at the door of evolution. It is also that which chains a forgotten Christ.

You have to choose in your reality every day what to do, what you think is right. But if you think in terms of right and wrong then you'll always do what is right. But it will never be good enough because the wrong has to come into play because it is a polarity; the two make a

The Nature of Reality — Morning Session

whole. So if you're doing things right, you're going to experience them wrong because the ideal in consciousness is separated by the polarity of right and wrong. You think good thoughts but they turn out so rotten; get it?

Now it's that simple. I'm not standing here this day saying in this one day you have to make the decision to evolve. This school was made up of days of progressive expression, progressively embracing the abstract, to stretch and to burn away the image in a day! It is incredulous to think this day you have to make the decision. "I'm burning it away; that's it. Forget it, I'm gone — out of here!"

But as Francis and as the Ram, the consciousness has to begin to appear and the voice within has to begin to become audible; it has to speak to you. When you start to listen is when you begin to change your reality. That's called "living your truth."

And what you do may be irresponsible, neglectful, unloving to other people but what do they know about love? You have to do what you feel you must do according to this voice that says, "Wake up! I'm in here! We have to do this! Do this with no regret. It will take you home — home. It will illuminate you. You talk of love; let's experience it." The Ram heard the voice on the rock; Francis, laying on his back dragged by his horse to a pond; Yeshua ben Joseph, making the choice at five.

Now then it begins to change the reality. You see, you have to want to; that's the key. And the want has to supersede the image because if you run the want through the image, all of the lights go on and it has a lot of fear. "I can't do that, can't handle that. I don't want to deal with that; it's too much. Give me something to meditate on." But then it starts to come alive! And as it begins to expand you and as this mind begins to awaken, very physical things begin to happen to the body. Very remarkable things begin to happen to one who begins to expand and their reality begins to change.

Don't you know what the fire is all about or the friction? Don't you know what all the pain is about and the ridicule and all of that? That was that great reality getting too big for its breeches, getting too big for all of the other realities attached to it! You're making waves when you begin to grow! And unless they grow with you, it's going to be a lot of pain to pull away from it all. But that is part of the choice of reality.

You will never experience again what you've already owned, never. And in the abstract, the mind of God, you'll never repeat anything. And in its beauty comes from knowing who you are. You don't need everything out here to say this is you, because the imageless being knows who it is and all the power comes home to the creator here, within.

Can your life change? Yes. How grand is your want? As grand as you perceive it. Is there more than what the eye can see? Yes. Don't you know why you can't see lights? And if most of the people in your reality can't and all of a sudden people are starting to come into your reality that do, it means that you're on to something because very shortly you'll be able to see what they see. That is growing.

And how is someone who can't see lights; where are they in evolution? Not very far. Because you can talk a big game, but if you can't see it and you haven't experienced it, you're not there because there is more to what is not seen. And that's what awaits you in the choice, in reality.

Listen. Think about it. Look how far you've come! Look at the changes you've made in your life. Look at where you're going. And there's one part of you on the surface that says this is for the birds. You're right; it is. And there's a part inside that is feeling very sovereign about life; that's the part that you listen to.

Now reality. Why don't you change your mind and just see your excuses? Because you made them. Don't you know that thinking in the abstract doesn't mean that it's void of an emotional experience? The emotion is when you have an experience with the abstract created in consciousness and manifested through the energy.

Listen you! Why must everything in your life depend on the "bottom line?" What kind of life are you living? If that isn't it, you're never going to hear a genius thought. You're not even going to get to know what your possibilities are, what your potentials are. And more than likely you're never going to see any lights because if you can't sell it, it ain't worth seeing! Get the point?

So where is your reality now? Stripping this all down to saying that you're the same as Yeshua ben Joseph is a big thing to say. And your little monkey-mind is going, "No, you're not! He's just giving you a line! You'll never be that good! You've already sinned. You've had two kids. You've had a few affairs. How could you be like Yeshua ben Joseph? He never had any woman in his entire life! At least that is what I was told." I have just reenacted an entity who was arguing a person's right to be Christ. And that is the monkey-mind speaking. Do you understand?

THE NATURE OF REALITY — MORNING SESSION

It is choice. It is desire. It is to see it as so, then it will be so. A person who has never had a spiritual experience doesn't want one. Because all they wanted is to prove it didn't exist really. Understand? Do you understand? And if you're drawing the same lover into your life and you're going through the same thing again, it's trying to tell you something about your reality: Change it!

And if indeed you're convincing yourself all of the time that none of this is working, you're going places because you're burning away the image and the hardest battle comes at the end. The last stroke of the broadsword is when the body heaves its greatest lunge at the enemy. And during the last moments of battle does the battleax have the most violent strokes. And the last moment of enemies in battle, at the last few moments — when the end is coming rapidly and you know one is going to die in this battle — the fight becomes the hardest. So it is in reality and change.

Now at a greater level this character, this altered ego that you're living, you should have absolved it 35,000 years ago. Do you understand? It's the same character every lifetime that has not evolved because it is stuck. It is stuck in the groove. That groove should have been one spin in the spiral called life instead of being the repetition of what is civilization. Do you understand?

These dilemmas that you're having — people, listen to me! This is the key to overturning all things. The consciousness that you create your first steps with, the Lord God of your being, that has brought rosiness to your cheeks and a song in your heart, took that and then manifested it and glorified you with the courage it took to do that. You haven't realized that you have to learn from that first step not only courage but what you have gained and what you have owned, that every change in your life you have to evaluate it as such. And the moment you begin to evaluate it you are stretching your consciousness more, because to every experience lies an unknown probability. It is the unknown probability of every experience that resolves what you have just created.

Because most of you think, "I have done this now." And after a while it begins to smell and nothing is happening. You can't go on to the next step because you're blocked, because you haven't increased consciousness to increase your reality to see what it is you've gained from that experience! There should be no problems in evolution. There should only be consciousness creating, absorbing another thought from the unknown, manifesting it into reality, experiencing that manifestation, creating reality and writing it in the book as wisdom. "We have experienced this." And you go to the next and to the next and the next, instead of getting hung up in your problems. There are no problems! There are only wisdoms yet to be earned. Get it? Get it?

Now in the ancient schools all of this would have taken days. And every day would have been based on five sentences and the rest of the day would have been working with consciousness to own every sentence — every moment, to have heard the word and then contemplated upon the word and stretched one's being to embrace it. That's why in the school of enlightenment you graduated. Everyone did.

But here it's sentence upon sentence upon sentence, trying not to bore you or to tire you, but get you to wake up and listen, that the whole year will be filled with every sentence, embracing and learning and moving through the density of doubt.

Now you're not going to learn anything that is not next on the agenda to learn, because every page of the seven pages has a whole list of experiences in which to engage an illuminated consciousness and manifest it; it's your duty to manifest it. And then when you're at the bottom of the page, like magic you wake up one morning and nothing is the same; there is a new person looking out of the window. That's because the page has turned in the book. You owned it all.

Now are there civilizations that have learned the simplicity of the nature of reality and left? Yes. They're long gone. Are you here to say that all that you've learned, that in all the lifetimes what you keep repeating was simply a conscious creation in which you could glean an experience from? And isn't it time to go on and get out of the rut? Yes? Like your brothers before you who have recognized who they are in a world of chaos, so you are to do. Your thinking as social consciousness is based on your image. Your thoughts on God are based on how you live it.

Reality. In my life, I am my life, for all things in my life bespeak of my consciousness, my mind. And all of my wisdom — yes, yes, my well of wisdom — whence say you it comes? I am gifted with this? Nay, nay, I have earned it. Every golden apple in that well I have earned. Pray, how did I earn being so wise? Alas, I have lived every experience and that has given me the jewel to understand. And so the bounty of my life is growing every moment beyond its perimeters be-

THE NATURE OF REALITY — MORNING SESSION

cause I do not cease to understand or engage, for I am a warrior of the truth within me. And then say you think I am beautiful? That I am. Say you think I am courageous and knowledgeable? That I am. But that which I am, or what you have perceived, is the beginning of what you will be tomorrow. So be it.

All you have to do is dream. All you have to do is contemplate and dare to contemplate. And all you have to do is to be grander to what you perceive yourself to be. And every moment you perceive it so the fantasy manifests as truth. Don't be weak; be strong. Don't see yourself as helpless; be abundant. Money, gold, establishment does not mean you are anything. It is what is within you that is everything.

There is more to the unknown. There is genius; there is probability; there is a reality far different from the one that you know now as to be you. There is a morning coming, some morning when the page will be turned and the image will be gone forever. And this that you are can walk over hill and dale and, yes, sleep under a great tree and be a light unto all people. Or you can live in a fine palace and look out its windows and look upon a world and find it beautiful, loving and kind. It is not the palace that makes you; it is your reality. It is how you perceive in consciousness.

Woe, don't look at your problems as problems! See them as unresolved experiences. Resolve them! They'll give you up. See your reality as ever-increasing! And if your altered ego gets bruised — it should take a beating in this trip — it is all right. It will bring you closer to creating that which you want, what you said to me. Yes, what is it that you said? "I want to be God; I want to be all that I can be; I want to have joy; I want to have wisdom and knowledge and then happiness; I want to be free; I want to ascend." Live first! Live! If death is the moment of awakening, then change awakens you! You are just beginning to live! Why ascend when it's just getting good? Yes!

"I want knowledge." Yes, so be it. All there is is there for the asking. Don't ask and on one hand fill your moments with noise and people and entertainment, where you block out your ability to receive. Don't you know that in the great, quiet silence of space lies unknown mind? How can you hear genius in the midst of chaos? If you want knowledge, go for it. If you want joy, it is the reality now to have it. That is your next step! And if you want happiness, don't you know it's your next step? Because if you were happy, you wouldn't have ever had to ask for it.

And all it is is choice, conscious choice. The biggie here — that is the biggie — is getting beyond the image. But guess who created the image? You did. What was it for the Ram to give up being the Ram? Seven years of pain, all of my life. And what humiliation it is to be accused by your army that you're weak. I know how quick followers can turn on their heels. Never be a leader; it's a dangerous job.

But it was seven years, seven years of understanding, and when I got off the rock I was not the Ram. My people could not see me any other way than as the Ram because they had not sat on the rock! They had not the hunger; they had not the desire to change a reality. They didn't even know what that meant! They were looking for home, and men thinking of alabaster knees, and children thinking of gleeful moments, and women thinking of babes in arms and corn in the field. Listen. They could never have understood me. They determined that I was the Ram but I was sick, because I was not the Ram they could identify with; I had changed. But that was my reality. I just wanted it. Do you understand? So what does it take? For a great barbarian to be humiliated by a pain in his back and people whispering at safe distances and saying what they had to say and conspiring, that burned away the image.

Now in the nature of reality we are only at the place we perceive to hold on in being. If we deny ourself the metamorphosis of glory, then you will forever be the caterpillar and never the butterfly with oriental fans of brilliant design. A stagnated spiritualist works on positive/negative, dark and light, and those are their excuses not to evolve.

I'm made of the same energy that Hitler was made of, Genghis Khan and Yeshua ben Joseph and Buddha Amin. It's just choices in evolution. And you have it all right here.

No, you never try to be something you're not; be what you are. That will be a new experience. Yes, changing is fearful. What it means is the image has no control over the unknown. No, there is no evil in the unknown. That's on pages three, two and one. No, if it doesn't make you happy to change and you make everyone in your life unhappy, then what you're saying about everyone in your life is that they really represent you. You don't want to change. That's all right. You don't have to. No one says you have to.

When you're ready to evolve it will burn in you like a flame; then

THE NATURE OF REALITY — MORNING SESSION

you'll know. Then you are evolving. Then you have been following these footprints as grandly as if I could have done them myself. And if you have fears, well, that's only natural in a state of change. I want you to know something: You are as eternal as I am. And when this little number is up, you'll see just what you have gained in reality, in your consciousness, when you leave this place. It's all eternity. It is an illusion because it is not fixed. The only thing that is real is nature. Problems are experiences created by consciousness to increase consciousness to solve them; therefore they are illusions. Don't ever give up on you.

Now what I'd like to prepare from my end of this teaching are runners based from my consciousness as to what I perceive what your want is. I can drum them up very nicely. So what you want at this point you are not capable of creating yet. But I can, based in your own image. I want to send you an experience of what you want from the abstract, that you can experience it so completely in a moment that it will give you the courage to go to the second year of understanding. Because there are Lords of Lords and Gods of Hosts that have the power to create that because they have earned it, your greater dimensions. So I wish to send to you this year an experience of what you want, to help reflect your lack and fill it up. So be it.

Because there's more to life than this reality. There is more to understanding than the repeating stuff you're doing. There is more to experience than just idle words. Don't be the philosopher; be the God. Get it? So be it.

Now it is time to break. Even in the ancient schools you learned how to manifest lunch! It is only at the seventh level of the seventh year can lunch be manna — and manna is knowledge. And there are beings that live in this level of your galaxy that don't eat. Their whole life — and they do live a long, long time — is based on knowledge. They've evolved to live off manna.

Well, you're not there. And there's nothing like good, hot, steaming porridge to make a person feel good about what he learned this day. You take these moments and you eat and be festive about what you eat. And don't sit there nitpicking, griping and complaining and bitching about what you're eating. Be thankful for it because the more thankful you are about your meager bounty, the more likely it's to increase. Now that could mean a lot of baloney or a lot of meaty

The Ancient Schools of Wisdom

joint — however you've seen it, of course.

And you rest and contemplate what you heard this day. And contemplate just what you heard this morning. And if you put it in your own words, you'll begin the process of owning it. And when you are done, you come back here. We've got to do a P.S. to this teaching. And do try to remember, those of you who are conscious in this time-space matrix, this is an ancient teaching that took a whole year to go through every line. So if you feel a little pressed towards time, maybe your next runner should be to reevaluate its value to you. So be it.

★

THE NATURE OF REALITY

AFTERNOON SESSION

Indeed! I am very happy to be here! I have to acknowledge you all that you may exist in my reality! So be it! Let's have something to drink.

*To you
And the God that you are.*

You contemplated? You are stretched?

Let's get on with it. So how was your reality over lunch? Did you learn?

Now you came here and the sky was very threatening, eh? And there was some of you that said "No, thanks" and some of you didn't care. You just wanted to be here as long as you were sheltered and you dressed warmly. That is allowing nature, living in harmony and still pursuing reality. So thumbs up to you! It's like a long march, and I appreciate you being here.

Now that also stretched you into increasing your consciousness because you made a commitment. It didn't matter that the skies were very dark and threatening; you just wanted to come and hear. Just by desiring to hear, you will gain because it will stretch your consciousness to absorb a new understanding, but really a forgotten one. So already you're winners before I ever opened my mouth. And that is a salute to the God that you are. So be it.

(*Aside to someone in the audience.*) Well, how are you doing?

The Ancient Schools of Wisdom

You're doing wonderfully? You learned? Indeed what think you reality is? *(I think it is what my life is, my consciousness that I'm living in right now, what I've created.)* And what is unreality? *(Probably the unknown that I haven't experienced yet; not in my perception in my reality.)* Do you think it ever will be? How do you know that? *(Because I know all things are possible.)* But possibility is conjectural — but conjecture also exists in the unknown. Correct? Do you think you'll experience the unknown? *(I know I will.)* Give me five!

Now what about this unknown business? Yes! That's what we want to get down to! Yes! So you think you know it all, do you? Want to get on with the unknown, do you? Yes? Aren't you scared? Well, you should laugh! After all, being God is pretty funny!

Now you know, you understand that the word God be that which is termed the ultimate power. And it's the exquisite word that means ultimate being, creator, divine essence. So you wrap it all up. You take all of eternity and put it in one word called God. So to say God is the epic expression of something that is quite divine, wonderful; it explains everything! "Well, God created it. Well, that's in God's mind and only God would understand why this does this."

Do you understand why I call you God? Because the awakening is yet to happen in the massive mind that you think is God. The subconscious mind is simply that: subconscious. It's asleep. It is yet to be made active. And that mind is the extension of what forever is all about. That which is awakened in the mind is the active God. And the active God is composed of consciousness and energy. And that is exactly what you are. You have the power to create because you are awake.

And it is indeed your destiny to awaken the entire mind. Heavy duty! You see why it's not altogether the most exquisite thing to tell a person that their destiny in this life is to be a hairdresser or to even be king! That's falling short of a most grandiose destiny! "Well, you don't understand, my destiny is not to be king; it is to be God and all that that means."

"I see."

"Well, I certainly hope you do! It will make a lot of things easier if you were to see instead of me doing all the seeing. You could at least share with my understanding of what I'm talking about here." Well, such is the conversation heard over lunch!

Now understanding the unknown. Well, let's talk about that. When

THE NATURE OF REALITY — AFTERNOON SESSION

I said to you that this plane — that which is termed coagulated thought, which is mass-to-mass, which is developed and evolved through the time-space matrix — this is the only level that you deal with time. From where I come is eternity. But today, as it wanes on, we are manifesting a year. Confusing, isn't it? I'm eternity in eight hours! And I make eight hours into a year. Confusing, eh?

Now why does it take so long? And why does a God get entangled with flesh and forget who they are? So why do you sit there, doubting that consciousness and energy constitutes that you are a living God? Why are you sitting there doubting with arms folded that you're more than a mere mortal? Because you have lost the ancient wisdom that is a truth bearing the standard of who you are in a journey on this level called mass. And in mass the God, at the twinkling of an eye, does not roll out the universe. That God, in the twinkling of an eye, must conceive the thought through that which is termed the workings of manifested density, which be that which is termed the body. Then it has to go through the process of feeling that identity. And then the next moment it has to make up its mind if it likes the feeling of that identity. And if it does, it flows out of the entity and begins to create in time the pieces of the puzzle that constitute the feeling of that manifestation. And it may take a year!

So what happened to the glory of a great God who could set thunder rolling into space, that all of a sudden is as helpless as his body is, that can have great thoughts, that can lift you to the pinnacle of heaven, only to open your eyes and realize it's time to relieve your body? What about this God?

Don't you understand that the ancient wisdom was preserved in a simple truth so you would never forget about the book that was created in involution — meaning in spirit to be lived through flesh, time, space, distance, this depth, this plane — the Book of Evolution. That when it was created this God would forget who they are. The ancient wisdom has been kept burning because in this body it's very easy to conclude that when you blink your eyes nothing happens. Then you must not be God; it must be a cruel myth. You're only as good as you feel you are; you're only as strong as your back is. And you can only pull so much of this world according to the yoke you put around your neck. How could that be God? How could you be that?

Why are you taking this journey through this time? Why are you taking this journey through this slow mass? Do you know? Think about it. The food that you just consumed, your body creates the energy to burn, to break it down so that it can feed itself with the gases to every cell. And what you consumed will soon be wastes, byproducts of energy, and that takes time to happen. Everything works in time here.

So if you were really God you wouldn't have to put up with that! The point is that's the myth. Because if you're God then every moment is the adventure to understanding that. And that every manifestation in time is the opportunity to grow and to experience it, to move through the density.

What do you think your cells are? Do you think they just came from the earth? Do you think they just came from your mother's womb, your father's loin? What do you think that is? It's the life force! And what is the intelligence in the life force? 'Tis you, who set it into motion! Everything is God! It is from the awakened God's reality who created it. But you get lost, see. You think you should do it just like that. And if you don't want to do it just like that, you want to ascend and get it over with!

ime; now let's talk about that. Because the P.S. in the nature of your reality, the truth is the nature of reality would not exist without the time flow.

Now you're going to have to picture this in your mind, so you're going to have to think a little bit. You're going to have to wake up. And you're going to have to create a vision of a spiral. Do you know what a spiral looks like? If you don't, I'll send you one. And take the spiral and turn it parallel to the ground, just have it go on and on and on and on, just sort of suspended there.

Now when people are stuck in the groove, they keep repeating according to the laws of their image. And they keep going in a circle. Now if you take a circle and begin to pull it this way, what do you have? *(Spiral.)* Yes. The time-matrix of space, quantum time, is viewed as a spiral.

Now I will explain how this works for your truth. In the spiral, as it begins at the top of the curve of time, there is a flash. And the flash is consciousness, and that consciousness creates matter. Matter; in the blinking of an eye, consciousness has manifested matter.

Now as the spiral turns a full circle it blinks again consciousness, which is matter. So you're going down time, and every evolution of that spiral, making the top circle, it blinks consciousness/matter. Now

THE NATURE OF REALITY — AFTERNOON SESSION

the opposite of the circle is also created and that is antimatter and subconsciousness.

Now think about the spiral and the circle. The top of the circle is consciousness; the bottom of the circle is subconsciousness. The top of the circle is matter; the bottom of it is antimatter. They are both equal to states of awareness.

Now in time you consciously absorb the thought and it becomes conscious. Flash! You're at the top of the spiral; you have an idea. The next moment that idea begins to make an evolution; it begins to turn. As it begins to turn, there is another flashing at the bottom from antimatter/subconscious mind. At that bottom will become the realization of the flash of matter. In order for consciousness to be there, there must be subconsciousness. In order for matter to exist, there must be antimatter.

Now time is creating the revolutions of the spiral that allow you to have a constant, as you term, consciousness. Now the top is consciousness; the bottom is subconsciousness. The top always is consciousness and matter. The bottom is always subconscious mind and antimatter. Now why would subconscious mind be on the bottom end of time? Because it is where consciousness is derived from. And why would matter be on the top and antimatter on the bottom? Because it takes antimatter for matter to be created from.

Now let's have a simple demonstration. Open your eyes very wide. Now find a point and look at it. Now I want you to do this: Blink your eyes very fast. Got it? Now every moment of your conscious life is only when those eyes are open; that's consciousness. Every moment that you don't see is subconscious mind and antimatter. You are working on consciousness and subconsciousness simultaneously. And all you realize is consciousness.

This life of yours is like this. If you take the spiral and stop the spiral and take it like a piece of film, you'll see the beginning of your life and you'll see the end of your life. And you can hold it still. And each frame is those changes in this life and you can look at them. But between each frame there is nothing, except it is the nothing that you created the changes from.

Now time is like a spinning wheel of film. And every moment that you are living in evolution, the moment that you create from subconscious mind into consciousness, you begin the spiral which is moving down the reality of that manifestation into frequencies, to levels of vibrations. When it hits the bottom at antimatter and subconscious mind is when it begins to materialize in your life. Then it comes back up and it has gone through seven levels of vibration to become the next blink.

Now this is profound stuff that I'm trying to make it simple here. The point I'm saying to you is that in order to manifest in time through mass you have to work with mass according to consciousness. If you understand that consciousness is the awakened part of the subconscious mind, then you must have both in a spiral of time flow in order to manifest reality. Because when you can blink your eyes like that, you are seeing the subconscious giving credibility to consciousness. So you're working off both minds.

Now it takes one full spiral to realize the "blurp" of conscious matter, to become realized conscious matter. And the bottom, where subconscious/antimatter bloops, is what creates it for the next realization. You go one whole spiral in time to manifest.

It's like this: You pull out an abstract thought and you're on. Your head is forward and you're on. And you are stretching consciousness. And the thought from nowhere comes into your being and you hold onto the thought. You begin to contemplate the thought. And as you begin to contemplate the thought you are lowering the thought because the body is heating up. Energy in the body is temperature change and as it begins to take on design, the body begins to get hotter and hotter. What has happened is that conscious matter is now in a spiral of creation; it is being created. It is being lowered all the way to this time flow that it can be created in the next blurp of reality. When it is released, the next frame in your life will be the manifestation of that abstract thought. And that is reality in the spiral.

And you have to have time in order to evolve it. But as the entity turns those pages in the book, they begin to unify consciousness to where subconscious mind is conscious mind. They begin to unify that which is termed matter with antimatter. They begin to unify that which is termed the layers of vibration because on every page that you come to, the energy begins to flow and there is nothing but now. And that is the journey of evolution through mass.

Time; yes, it is imperative for the journey. It is imperative. It is what is indicative of this journey through mass back to the Godhead realized, illuminated! But you have to work with time in order to understand matter.

Now you're sitting here trying to think! And you don't want to act dumb, so you're trying to look intelligent. But you're sitting here and you're looking at me and I look very constant and you're thinking, "He has been talking now for twenty moments" and you've seen me constantly. You don't understand that all you're reacting to is consciousness. All you're reacting to is matter because you don't see those spaces in between the frame. And you don't realize what sort of time has passed because you're seeing matter only as a constant. It is not constant. Every moment, every space between the frame of those twenty moments, there is eternity. And eternity is called now and that mind is constant. But all you see is a continuum, an uninterrupted flow of twenty minutes. And you haven't understood the eternity between those twenty moments, that moment when the bloop is antimatter/subconscious mind. But it's pressing to you every moment.

In the twenty minutes of this spiral we have created an eternity, in twenty moments, by simply captivating the essence of what this time flow is all about and how it works.

Now I use the spiral to get you out of the circle and to pull you forward to evolve. It's imperative you understand about matter and antimatter, as well as consciousness and subconsciousness. They are both equal because it is from the subconscious that the conscious is made stable. It is from antimatter that matter is created because antimatter exists in subconscious mind. Talk about the nature of reality! You've seen twenty minutes go by but I am concentrating on those instances between the frames, all of those possibilities and how they got there.

Now to expand — and your destiny is to expand consciousness that the handmaiden of energy can manifest it, that it can create a reality that is ever-growing, ever-increasing in your life because they work as magical instruments.

But how does it work? You can't simply say, "I'm going to stretch my consciousness and therefore it's going to manifest and it will take two weeks or twenty moments." You have to know how it works because when you know how it works, you will own the understanding of time. And you will own the sense of constant reality that makes you old instead of being that still frame in between that is all power, mind. The spiral is time; it has to go through every sequence, through seven levels. Everything that you expand upon in consciousness has to be designed through seven levels of thought waves, frequencies, energies, levels of vibration. They have to fall down those degrees in reality in order to manifest in this level. And that takes time.

Why? Because the moment that you have matter/consciousness — it's like a blurp — the moment that you embrace it, it has to start its downward fall. It falls seven levels in vibration to get to its polarity at the bottom of the circle. Then it hits, bloop, antimatter/subconscious mind. And from that the materialization of what you created in consciousness will occur on the next top of the spiral. And blurp, it will be reality that you have just expanded. That's how it works.

Your life is blurp, blurp, blurp. Subconscious and antimatter is bloop, bloop, bloop. I want you to understand the bloop, what you are not hearing, what you're not seeing because you see only matter.

You see, consciousness creates matter, people! Don't you understand? The nature of reality is based on consciousness. And so in the time-matrix of space in the spiral, only matter will be perceived by you because that is what your consciousness is! I'm trying to get you into the bottom of the spiral to understand how you manifest the law of whatever you think is. And the moment that consciousness is working into new fields of adventure, it is pulling from that which is termed subconscious mind. Every moment you're sitting there contemplating, those blurps are going, blurp, bloop. That engine is moving! All because consciousness is looking forward, stretching, embracing from the unknown, going into the depth to create great mind and then it starts cranking.

Now what about the person who says, "Yes, well, I'm this and I'm that and I don't need to learn anything else! I know where I'm at." They're going in a circle. Boring, boring, boring! There's no blurp, bloop, blurp; it's just a circle. Your consciousness keeps the reality of what you already know constant. That's your reality. There is no antimatter. There is no subconscious mind working in social consciousness. There's only recycled ignorance. It goes in circles over and over. And that's the reason why the entity doesn't see lights, they don't have profound visions, they don't walk out to a midnight sky and hold their hands up and light appears because they're going around in circles. They think they're moving forward but they're not. They're not activat-

THE NATURE OF REALITY — AFTERNOON SESSION

ing it. It's not happening. Now knowledge allows for you to move off the circle and begin to pull it, which creates the spiral of time. You have to have time to begin the realizations on page four in the Book.

Knowledge allows you to understand how consciously you live, how you create your reality. Your reality is the top of that spiral. It's all of those blurps. You only see that. I want you to see all of it, to understand that other mind, the antimatter and the magnetism that is created when you do this, when you start the mind moving.

Magnetism; it is a divine energy. You can't figure it out in physics because it is a phenomenon of creation. It is a phenomenon of time because the magnetism is the energy that is created when you begin to stretch this consciousness and it begins its descent into the spiral. It is given validity by subconscious mind/antimatter and it begins its ascent. That is the moment that magnetism is created in this manifestation. That is the power and the energy that you feel around a person; it is their magnetism, because they can pull up a thought and make it happen because it takes that to come to the next level of the spiral to go, blurp, "This is your reality."

But some of you are on the circle going round and round, not seeing any blurps, not understanding why it's taking so long. You're impatient people. In the time flow the wise person understands that in evolution on this level, to master this level and move through the density of mass, you must have time and you must discover its secrets. You must unify its frequencies and unify subconscious with conscious, matter with antimatter, that there will come a moment when the seventh seal, on the seventh day that everything is now, that you have unified consciousness/time, that you have collapsed the spiral into a blaze of light. That is when you are talking to a Christ, one who understands. And you only evolve to get to Christ through time and this space-matrix called the spiral. Get it?

Now what I just explained to you is very complicated. It is very intent. It would take you to own genius in physics and mathematics, to discover the equation $E=MC^2$; not to repeat it but to know it. But it is the beginning of unifying the fields of consciousness and time, this matter.

In your reality you look around your bubble. You're sitting in the center; you gaze around your bubble 360 degrees and it looks like one sweep. The point is that all you're seeing is the blurps; you're not

… seeing what's creating it. I am telling you that what's creating it is the unseen God that is within you. It is the energy that takes the thought and materializes it.

You look around and you don't see any interruption in your little game. The point is that's all you can see. And you say, "It takes a long time for me to do this." Then you have set yourself up to achieve that three blurps down the way. And you won't create anything until you have accomplished those blurps on the spiral.

Now did you just understand what I said? Do you know how you plan your calendar? Do you know how we know that next year is going to come? Because you have a lot of appointments. You've scheduled those things to happen; therefore reality has to occur so you can take care of business. Do you understand?

Well, when you set goals for yourself, you set them according to the spiral in time. How many blurps down the way? You're going to have to do this, then you can do that, then you can do this and pretty soon you're close and then you can graduate. That's ten blurps down the way. And you cannot manifest anything else until you have manifested that goal because you have put the block out there.

Now you have to do everything you can in order to achieve that blurp! So you set yourself up in the spiral downturn. The only thing you're going to glean from the downturn is that you've got to accomplish the goal ten blurps away. You won't accomplish anything else. Take your calendars out and pick a date. Say, "This date I'm going to be alive." And you will stay alive until that date. After that we don't know, of course. Take your calendar out and pick out something you want to achieve on a certain day, or a miracle. "On the autumnal equinox a miracle will happen to me." Now where is that on your spiral? Well, it depends on if you're a circle or a spiral. If you're a spiral, it's approximately five blurps down the way and the miracle is going to happen that day.

Mm-mm, blurp, mm-mm, bloop, mm-mm, blurp, mm-mm, bloop, mm-mm, blurp, mm-mm, bloop, mm-mm, blurp. "By Jove, I just saw a light in the sky!"

"By golly, I just got healed! How wonderful!"

"I just saw my dead mother! She looks younger than ever!"

Do you understand what you just did? Now we're talking reality here in time. You created a reality in time that had to manifest! You try it. You pick a day out in your future and say, "This day I'm going to

THE NATURE OF REALITY — AFTERNOON SESSION

have a miracle." Do it. I would make it close up, if I were you.

Now whatever you've done, you've insured the spiral because it is waiting to happen. It is already created. And all of the blurps up to that point will be lived for that miraculous day. Don't believe me? Try it.

Now at the moment you did that you just pulled from subconscious mind and antimatter all that it would take to design it in consciousness, that every revolution in the spiral will go to make it the highlight of your life, and it will happen.

Now a lot of other things aren't going to happen in between them because you are living for the future rather than for the now. Do you understand? Wake up! Now think about this spiral in time. Now if you can figure this one out, just like I said, you will own time. And the moment you have owned its mystery, everything will speed up in your life. So be it.

Now you think about what I just said to you as simply as I could and you figure out the blurps and the bloops. You think about everything constant, matter vs. antimatter. You get it real straight in your mind. If you can visualize what I have just told you, then the next moment that you sit down to work with abstract consciousness you will know exactly how it will materialize in time. And you'll own its mystery. And the next moment you sit down to do it, the manifestations will start to quicken where one day all you have is to think it and it is.

Just look at a circle sideways. Where have you been? *(In the groove of the circle.)* Yes. And the desire is to change, and the next rotation is out of the groove — virgin, unknown, untried, nothing familiar. The conscious desire to change took you out of the groove. And the exalted feeling that happened, happened at the bottom and it went this way. That was the bloop of subconscious mind. You have just touched the mind of God, sleeping all-known intelligence. And at the moment antimatter blooped, the creation for a new life was set and the magnetism was going back up on the next rotation. And the next blurp in consciousness is its illumination and its manifestation. It has already achieved it in the soul. And in the next moment that you stretch out consciousness, you're in it again. You touch subconscious mind; you dip into it and through the magnetism carries it up to have created it in the next rotation. And every move into space and the inertia, the vacuum calls you forward.

THE ANCIENT SCHOOLS OF WISDOM

The spiral isn't already there; it's created in time. And every move out is unlimited thinking walking the unknown. And every moment you dare to live as a now human being, every moment you dare to expand consciousness, you are in the spiral of time controlling a reality just the way you want it because that reality is empowered to you by the energy coming from subconscious mind. And antimatter gives the credence to matter in consciousness, the magnetism. And every rotation is evolution. And in every rotation the pages in the book are turning. And everything is being recorded with every blurp that is realized from subconscious mind. It is being written in the book. You're having experiences and adventures and you're wanting more, and the mind is activated and you're on the spiral roll! And the more you understand about this, the smaller the spiral becomes. Until one moment there comes just a beam of light; that is your destiny. So be it.

Materialism is God, too, but it is only the clay that one manifests for the purpose of gaining a learning from, an expression from. It isn't the ultimate prize in this spiral, this time experience. It is the necessary element that forges a barbarian into a living God, that forges a primitive mind into divinity.

It's not what you manifest; it's that you did it. It's not how big or how small of what you manifest; it was that you did. The prize in accomplishment is not materialization; it is its accomplishment, which means growth. And every accomplishment means another blurp in the constant of who you are. That's growing.

You could live every day off of the accomplishment of self, of the expanse of knowing who you are, of taking on the challenge of becoming greater every day, of opening a mind up that's so rhythmic, so attuned, it has aligned itself and rapidly changes and grows; a chameleon of truth. You could live every day if you knew that every day would bring you an accomplishment of what you manifested in consciousness. It doesn't matter how large your feast is or how small; it's what you accomplished.

All of this time is necessary. One day it will not exist. There comes a day when what you want to see is not the frame in the film but the spaces in between. Do you get it?

Now when you're in the circle, to tell anyone's demise or their future is very easy to do, for a sage can take the circle and undo the film, see the beginning, see the end, make it stand still. And anyone that's up on anything, just the least little bit, can figure out this person's

THE NATURE OF REALITY — AFTERNOON SESSION

future because it's repetitive. That's easy to do. Now it's when you're in the spiral that you can't do that. Because everything at the end of that spiral is like those blank spots in between the frames. Get it?

Now time. Well, in my day I didn't wear a watch; I didn't even have any. We had a water clock, but mostly it was the glory of the sun seen in the last days of my life, which hadn't been there always. At the time I thought it was a rotation of the sun around my world. I didn't know that my world was rotating around the sun. That was my time. Nonetheless, it was time. Well, why couldn't the Ram heal his wound in the days that he sat on the rock? Why did it take seven years? Because it took me seven years to burn away the image that was enslaved to time.

Well, I've said to you in the past, "Be. Know." That's a simple truth. "Allow. Just be now." Everything changes but now is the sweetest ever; now. What you couldn't understand is that the now that I spoke of was not the continuing blinking that you're seeing here that seems constant, but it is when you stop working with time and how you collapse its need. And you won't do that until you have evolved through it. And like everything in their time and season, you'll be born and you'll die as long as you're working through the time process ignorant of it. But when you understand it and own it, you will collapse it and now will be forever. But that's when the spiral collapses and becomes the beam of light. Do you understand?

Now, people, so what was the big P.S. all about? Don't you understand the "biggie" of what I just told you, how consciously you create your reality because your reality is this constant, uninterrupted show, the greatest show on earth, your life uninterrupted? That's all you see. That's your reality.

When you understand that how consciously what you are thinking, consciously what you are, you create. And all of those blurps on the top of that spiral are your reality. And what you perceive this moment is the next blurp, stretching, stretching. You're not going to be the same in the next blurp as you are now. You're going to move; you're going to change. The same power that it took to start the roll is not the same power of the magnetism that takes you to the top of the next one. Your consciousness is continuously expanding. You're changing. When you stop changing, you start going in a circle and repeating. And that's when you take your life because you hate your life.

Get off of it. Move. Every moment you're evolving, stretching. Every moment the consciousness is becoming greater. Every moment the reality is expanding. Every moment that which you desire and intentionally go after manifests.

When you understand the process of time and its need and its necessity here, you'll own it. And soon the spiral collapses and you say, "I am that which I am!" And the God has come forward in full measure.

So what about your reality? If you stay here, it's simple. We just unroll the film and I'll tell you when you're going to die or what you're going to do next year. If your whole life is based on everything that you think might happen, it's very predictable what's going to happen to you. If you start brooding into the unknown, that is unpredictable because then you are activating your unknown mind, and that adventure no one knows but you. Get it?

Now the nature of reality. "It's what I want it to be. I want to be happy! So I'm happy. I want to be sad and I deserve the right to be sad, so leave me alone! I want to cry in my brew, I deserve that. I worked hard to feel this way! And I'm not going to change to make you happy. I'm going to be happy being me. And I'm not going to be any different, just how I want to be. And I can't tell you I'll be here tomorrow. I don't know if I want to be! All I know is that whatever I desire in this next moment is my life, my reality." Get off being the victim. Take control of this, understand how your power is working.

And don't give me that guff about that if you do this, it's going to make everything else wonderful, because this is very powerful. But what you say when you get up is just as powerful. How you're acting by mid-afternoon is just as powerful. Do you understand? In saying, "I am God, I am God, I am God, I am God," is not going to make it any better when you say, "goddamn me."

Consciousness is creating it all, and everything counts in this game. And idle chatter counts because it makes you boring. Gossip counts because it makes you wickedly important. Everything counts! So don't sit here and say "So be it" to me and walk out that door and say, "I can't," because the duality will be that as the opportunity comes, you won't be able to do it. Both consciousnesses are manifesting in the spiral. You start to go forward and then you go round in the circle. Do you understand?

THE NATURE OF REALITY — AFTERNOON SESSION

And you can't say to me, "I want to be God!" By God, don't you know you already are? If you don't know you already are, well, you have to go back before this classroom ever started and go back to the rudiments: Who are you? Why are you here? Who were you in your past life? Talk to your higher self and it will give your lower self some comfort! Do you understand? Don't desire to be God! BE IT! In a moment, blurp, you are; it is. Get it? When you say, "I want to be happy," and then you say, "Mark it up, I AM happy, ha-ha! Ha!" Bloop, blurp. Yes! And who can laugh in the face of a hangman? "Ha-ha! Ha-ha! Take it off! Ha-ha!" A God, that's who!

And if you say, "I'm getting out of this rut!" No. "I AM out of this rut" bloop, blurp. And you go home and someone says, "I can't even identify with you anymore. You're not even the same person when you left here."

"Whew! I was hoping you would say that!" Yes!

"Something's happened to me!" Yes!

And you don't say, "I am worthy to be love." You say, "I AM love." Yes. Bloop, blurp, and it is.

And that which you create in your reality is equal to your desire to create it. Excuses, you know: "Well, I don't know about this. I don't feel right about calling myself God. I mean, well, you know, I have fecal gases! I just don't ever conceive God to have fecal gases! And I don't feel sort of right saying that. You know what I mean?

"They asked me for my license the other day and they asked 'What is your real name?' I almost said 'God' but I knew they wouldn't believe me, which only goes to prove that I don't feel so good about this. And not only do I not feel very good about this, the whole world doesn't feel good about that I should feel good about saying that I'm God. I'm having a little problem with this. Do you understand?"

I said, "But of course, indeed I do."

"You understand?" Yes, I do. Yes I do.

Well, if you don't feel good about that, then you'll spend all of these years in this audience wanting, but reflecting everything you learned in knowledge. "I want it, because I feel it's true. Ah! But I can't live it; it's too incredulous. I can't make those changes. That's a lot to ask from me! Commit myself? What's he talking about? Go and live like some backward farmer? You've got to be nuts! I'm supposed to do this, that's the price I pay? Ah, it's too incredulous!" But you come back for more. And you want it so much, but your consciousness won't allow you because you created the consciousness.

And when you just say, "God Almighty, I AM. From the Lord God of my being, that which I am, I am," this starts to roll and the lights start coming on and truth begins to flow like a river. And things are working. And all the frictions and all the pain and all the heartache, every rotation begins to own and to polish, and the light gets brighter and brighter.

Don't you know you're not the character? You're not your name in this life. You're not just a woman or just a man. Do you understand that it's not your Social Security number? You're not just that; don't you understand? It's not what you look like in the mirror; it's what you are. It's that powerful essence that's creating the reality. Don't let your image do it because you'll always stay here. You don't need someone; you need you. "Someone" is only a mirror of what you lack, and they let you see for a while who you are!

Where is self-love? That reality is waiting to be expressed. And when it comes out, it changes identities. You change. You have the option to change. You have to.

And in time every manifestation, every consciousness you embrace, everything, you take it to the limits. It will come around and happen for you. And the whole of your reality, the purer your thought, the more profound your reality will be.

Now the pure thought, what do I mean? Clean it up? No. Pure. I'm saying speak not as a stupid ignorant person but as someone who knows. Don't speak just to hear your tongue rattle; mean something when you say something, as if you're pulling it out of the core of your being, even a jest. I jest and I pull it out of the core of my being to jest, but I do it as pure Ramtha. Let it be pure you. Clean it up; pure.

Don't say on one hand, "I love that which I am," and then say to another, "I am not happy with myself." Do not create a duality, two lies to have to live, two realities that are in contention all of the time.

In the ancient school it took a year just to clean up thought. Instead of cursing yourself, don't ever curse yourself. Don't ever goddamn anything because whatever you do is going to come home to you. Get it? Because "goddamn" is as much a law as "God I am." Do you understand?

So in one year of the ancient schools, consciousness and energy

THE NATURE OF REALITY — AFTERNOON SESSION

was to burn away the superficial and get to the glory, to work in one moment, to hold an abstract thought and let it work through the body and heat it up and then release it. So be it. And then the next morning wake up and feel illuminated by it because you did. That's cleaning up.

Because it's not just what you say in this audience; it's what you say all the time. It's not what you think here; it's what you put your mind on all of the time. If you don't want to live on page two or page one, get out of the gutter and get on to looking forward. If you don't want to be bothered by indecent thoughts and temptations, stop looking at them. Because they are there because you manifest them to be there. Do you understand? And if you want to have a future, get out of your past.

The nature of reality is a now principle that begins moving the spiral forward. It doesn't back up and go in reverse; it begins now. And you're not going to move very far in front of you as long as you tag along yesterday's news! It isn't important who you were in your last life! It's dead and in the grave somewhere or at the bottom of the sea! It's who you are now, in here. And it's this moment that you move forward! So get rid of your past, own all of your mistakes, turn them into wisdom, clean out your closets, get rid of your filthy mouths and get your fingers off of your privates and start putting it in your heart and say, "From God, my being, come forth!" Don't go into the past; don't turn back the pages!

"I want page four. I want it! I want to know what it is to love unconditionally, what it is to begin the path of a Christ." That is where you start — now — in cleaning up you. It's how you begin. "I'm ready." You begin to change. Do you understand?

And listen, you! The nature of reality is now. If you're going to make your past now, then your past becomes your reality now. How can you ever have a tomorrow until you're free of it? In time you have the opportunity to manifest genius, brilliance, powerful love, to be flowing like a river of light, understanding melodies, words — oh, words! — poems, the magician, numbers, facts, realizations, colors, attunements — all waiting — levitation, owning gravity. It's all waiting out here! But you can't do that until you clean it up and start and turn around and look forward. That should be your reality.

I don't care what you did yesterday. I love you for what is in here waiting to come forward. You know, your characters are going to wrinkle. They are. They're going to grow old and all the illusions with them. But the light never dies.

The past has nothing to do with this God within. It has everything to do with the next page in evolution and reality. And how do you get there? Be now, now! No yesterday, no regret, no longing, no need to look back; just now. Because everything that was yesterday is the wisdom that allowed you to create a dynamic reality.

So how can you put all of your mind-focus on a miracle if part of it is caught up in being the glory that is long-dead yesterday? If part of consciousness is thinking of the bygone days or if it is sitting there feeling bad about its mistakes, if its focus is always there, what part of you is alive and well to create a nature of reality that is progressive and mind-expanding?

What part of you, people, is ready to encounter a light in heaven? What part of you is ready to leave your body and take a journey through time? What part of you is ready to levitate yourself from one space to another? What part of you is tired of being sick? What part of you wants to live instead of preparing to die? What part of you is ready to meet God in the adventure called life, if so much of it is focused on the "real" world?

Well, there's something wonderful that happens up here that's not on your telly or on your radio; they are programming of the most intense degree. If I were to make you prisoners and put you on a planet in the furthest part of the universe and keep you there, without any cell around you, I would program you through your media and I would keep you right where you are and never worry about you. Then I'd own you completely because you are only the reflection of what I tell you to think every day. "Good Morning America! The news of the world today doesn't look good. But thank God you're going to make it, at least through this newscast. And we have a special guest here to talk about what it is to be sexual. So stay tuned after this message." Is that how it goes? Yes? Yes, I know. I watch. I understand, eh?

Now what the world doesn't know is what you have locked up inside of you. What your doctors don't know is about this mushy organism here (the brain), this mass, that when you're born into this body it has only so many main avenues. And a person who lives in social consciousness only creates their avenues in the part of this brain that's activated so that they can follow a daily routine, to be civilized. They do it over and over again, the "highway" of the brain! Now that's all. And when you die at the end of the film, they cut open your brain

THE NATURE OF REALITY — AFTERNOON SESSION

and they slice it, and they go, "Hm. Ordinary person. That's it for you! You don't need to keep this brain! It didn't do anything! Bury the sucker; get rid of it!"

Now evolving. The moment an entity embraces from the subconscious mind, things happen in this brain. The pituitary gland, you know it? It sits between the hemispheres. The want makes it bloom. It blooms into what looks like a flower called a lotus. And out of the bloom comes a hormone flow that begins to activate another part of the brain that dictates electrical current. And that part of the brain makes inroads into the brain of this electrical current and impresses onto up-to-then dead mass and makes it alive; it creates new "highways." And the thought coming in begins to travel down these highways. Electrical current fills the body with an exceptional high, and the soul starts recording the heat that is coming from this thought, that is pressing through brain mass to be realized in the body. And as it is being heated up, it's going down in a circle. And the magnetism is happening and the "jazz" happens. You're getting closer and closer, and the next moment you know you have realized the thought completely. The lights are on! Blurp!

Now do you know what you did to your brain? You created a new brain with just one thought! Now in the next moment you turn around — "Forget the past! Let's do this! Yes!" — and another great thought comes! It does the same thing. The mind starts expanding and pulsating, the body starts heating up, and the thought has created another inroad into the brain. Genius is happening here.

Pretty soon the pituitary continues to get larger and larger and larger and the brain begins to be more activated. And the inroads of that great thought — the first thought, unlimited thought outside of social consciousness — its highway is still there, its marks are still there on the brain tissue, and pretty soon thought, highway, emotion, heat, hot, mm, reality, blurp! Mm, hot, highway, tissue, bloop, mm, blurp. You understand?

Now what begins to occur in reality — and your bubble is going mm-mm and all the little bubbles are going mm-mm-mm and there is a big bubble happening here — is a great God that's coming out who is "on."

And as it turns to page five, something wonderful happens. Because of all the highways that have been created in the brain tissue,

The Ancient Schools of Wisdom

something begins to happen. All of them then begin to merge at one central part of the brain that is right behind the ear, this little part in the rear of the head. They all begin to cross into this one section and this one section is an amplifier of tremendous magnitude. And at that point you start to see dimensions. What the eye does not see becomes visible: power; the intuitive is born in splendid birth; to look across a galaxy and pick up a thought; to be able to see the aura of the Ram standing in front of you; to be able to look around you to see another dimension; to look into tomorrow. It is the ability that sits right behind your ear, here. It is genius. It is more brilliant. The word is Christ. That happens starting at the fifth.

And one becomes so caught in traveling through this world into the dimensions that await to be experienced — not only down the road on the spiral but by the God inside coming forth — that this physical manifestation takes on the qualities of stigmata. It takes on the quality of healing hands. It takes on the quality of a God walking and moving without touching the ground. It takes on the quality of an illuminated being. And you know it. The power is absolute.

Every one of you have that part in your brain, every one of you. Because when this is completely exercised and the pituitary is in full bloom, that which is termed the brain is in full bloom and the highways have been completed in this expression, then behold Christ of the seventh level. And that's down on the spiral away.

So what happens when you pass away and someone wants to take a look at your brain? Well, they start slicing it up and they start seeing all of these ribbons of highways through a single part of tissue, a sure indicator that this person was brilliant. They were a thinker. They had reason. They had the tenacity to think, to be original. They contemplated and used that organism. No, they weren't just another person; they were an extraordinary person. And what about this mystery, this gland that's opened up completely? "What caused it to open? What did that person know that I don't know?" Want. So every highway was the path home. And every part of that path was the illumination and the continued expanse of reality.

How do you know the unknown exists? Most of you are afraid to change because you don't know what you are changing into. The image shows you how small your reality is. Don't you know every highway increases this bubble that you go beyond the

THE NATURE OF REALITY — AFTERNOON SESSION

common man and common woman? That your knowingness is acute, hot, sizzling, electric, powerful. It all comes from "I want to know. From the Lord God of my Being, I want to know. So be it."

Scientifically speaking, an enlightened person's mind can be proven. Unfortunately it happens after they die, but it can be proven. Reality, you know, has nothing to do really with what you're eating tonight or how much money you made this month. Reality has everything to do with an ever-increasing consciousness, a wonderment.

There are no questions in the universe; there's only life waiting to be discovered. And really a question is not, "Tell me the answer," but, "Can I find it myself?" Yes, that is evolution.

Whenever you look at a midnight sky and you find a Venus rising, contemplate it and see. Is that you, consciousness? Is that as big as your reality or is it larger? Well, you're only as big as you perceive yourself to be. So if you're going to be discreet and pick out the faintest, smallest, tiniest, wee, little star and you think that's dainty to do that, then that's a good indicator of how great your reality is. If you pick out the biggest, boldest light in the heavens, it's a good indicator of how great and arrogant you think you are and what kind of reality you are capable of creating. And that's wonderful.

So how did the nature of reality and the spiral of time and matter and antimatter make a hill of beans this day? Well, it's knowledge. You can make up all the excuses that you can for not being an enlightened entity, and it can take you the rest of your life to see yourself as such. Well, you can make it in one choice of pure desire of "I want," and with that want comes the energy to create the manifestation. You're as great as you think you are. You are as powerful as you think you are. And you have exactly in this life what you deserve. And you'll never have more or less than the point of consciousness that deserves it.

Now students of ancient wisdom, it would have been splendid to have had you in my audience for one full year in addressing this teaching, but it's still going to take you a year to understand what you heard this day. And it's not hard. The difficult part is getting rid of your complications, to get simple. Understand?

Now there's no superstition in this. There's no hope in this teaching. There's no dogma in this teaching. And we didn't set the world on fire with this because what I have just told you is not new. It is a cosmic law; it is the way that it is. It's just I thought you'd like to know that you can increase it. And that when I tell you to heal yourself, I'm not pay-

THE ANCIENT SCHOOLS OF WISDOM

ing you a compliment; I'm stating a fact.

And when I'm telling you, "You're creating your excuses," I'm not putting you off; I'm making you address them. And when I'm telling you, "Get sovereign," I'm not making you give up anything; I'm making you earn everything. And when I say to you, "Love what you are," I'm not telling you that to make you feel good; I'm saying that because in loving who you are, you touch the hem of the mind that made you.

The nature of reality. It can be anything you want it to be. You create the barriers.

Now knowledge. You are a much more enlightened audience now than you were earlier. You're not spiritually ignorant. You are becoming Godlike and wise. An answer shouldn't be the answer — it should be earned knowledge. It is far greater to have knowledge than the king's kingdom.

Well, the next moment you sit to embrace the abstract there's going to be a knowingness inside of you that goes, "Yeah, yeah, yeah, you're on! We can do it." And somehow there will be a patience that comes with this, too, because you'll understand time. And that everything you embrace must have its fall to be created in the subconscious mind. You're going to understand that!

You won't have to say this excuse, "Well, whenever it happens, it happens." That's a spiritual cop-out. You'll understand why; get it? And the next time you have a blurp you'll understand it's not so much of what you blurp, but it's what made the blurp. Understand? And then when we talk about the voice within, we're not talking about a demon or a demigod, we're talking about the imageless being that is controlling this entire drama, an entity waiting to emerge.

And when we talk about the identities, we're talking about all the things that are fearful and limiting. You'll understand. And the next time you're afraid to change, you'll understand where it's coming from. Do you understand?

Now if you want to change your life, get up and do something about it and start consciously changing a thought into that direction. The law is "Everything will follow." That's how it works.

I wanted to be the wind; I was. So if a bad-breathed barbarian can become the northern wind, just look at what you can do, civilized man.

So be it! That is all.

You contemplate what you have learned this day. I have a whole host of runners that will bombard you every moment you have some

quiet. And this teaching will not leave you alone. So be it.
That is all.
I love you! And that is my reality!

When you are living because you are happy and not because of changes, think of me. And if you want your reality to be like mine, I'm only a breath away.

The Destruction of Ancient Wisdom and Its Resurrection

Morning Session

Indeed! I love you. You pay a wondrous honor to me. And I do not forget; I am very grateful.

You will evolve to the fourth level — and some of you are already there — to where you discover a love of the glory of God that you are, that you love what you are. And inasmuch as that which has become precious to you, in your reality you will only see God in others. It is called unconditional love. And for you who evolve to that place awaits a kingdom that is rich in life, beauty, and the glory that is called forever. Such have I been. So when say I to you that I love you greatly, it is because what I see within you I have become myself. So be it.

Yes, let's have a drink.

In saluting the Lord God of your being you pay the highest tribute to what you are. In saluting life forever you recognize its importance to you who create its realities. So let's salute the Lord God of your being and life.

> *From the Lord God of my Being*
> *Unto the glory within,*
> *Unto my reality*
> *That I consume in life,*
> *May it glorify and reflect*

THE ANCIENT SCHOOLS OF WISDOM

> *The power,*
> *The beauty,*
> *And the Grace*
> *That the Lord God of my Being*
> *Surely is.*
> *To Life!*
> *So be it!*

Now we can get on with some knowledge.

To you pilgrims, some of you have come a long way, and not in distance but in evolution, to be here. You have conquered many things to come here. Primarily speaking, your altered egos. Pilgrims I call you because your adventure is not solitary and it's not standing still; it is ongoing. There is a restlessness in every entity who is living life to discover its entirety of who it is and its manifested destiny.

I do not look upon you lightly; I look upon you with all great sincerity. And I'm honored and pleased that such a host could gather itself and not for entertainment but because it wants to know. It hungers for knowledge to provide the window that it may go forward, and not being afraid, but wanting enlightenment, to enlighten the darkness of the not-knowing. That is what knowledge provides. It releases the chains and those things that harrow self, which is doubt.

Well, all of you here are important. There are some of you here that need desperately, desperately, to be recognized, to be acknowledged, to be touched, for being something special. It is a bruised soul that cries out for the need to interact, to fill up within yourself that which in your destiny you will fill from the imageless God within. And part of the reason that you have not evolved as rapidly for 35,000 years as you should have is that you have been bruised. A lack of self-esteem, which is the quantum of being important, being confused, creating diverse realities, they keep you separated from what you are. You should have moved on a long time ago.

Well, the concept of the teaching of what the Ram was, who came to say, "Behold God," which you are but nobody could hear because they wanted to be embraced and loved. They wanted to be loved back into life and feeling needed. They are lost and bruised souls, confused with the jargons of superstitious dogma, worshipping powerless beings. So all these years I have been sending runners, manifesting, trying to get you to move out of your boxes — not because it's more profitable gold-wise. I never taught you for the sake of money but for the sake of your soul to evolve. So all of the years I've been loving you constantly, steadfastly, to hold you up like little children and continue to shine light in dark and superstitious places, that you will see that only a wisp of an illusion existed, not a reality. And you had to be nurtured all over again to come back to a simplified truth, an assurance that that truth could bring, that would put you back on course on the path of your destiny instead of spinning you around in circles and creating a following or worshipers. People who need to be stroked go to gurus who need to have the power.

I'm very honored to be here. I've learned so much of how to communicate with you, how to talk, how to fling out your lingoes, so that the word could not be confused and idolized but clear, regardless of the pain, that it would heal within the soul a way that you could understand.

There's been a tremendous conspiracy for you for ever so long, and such a sleeping, as every human being has, that they are even programmed that they dare not wake up, reason or think or dare to be free.

To this small group — you're certainly not two million strong — the truth is like a flame and everyone who carries it is liken unto a lantern in the night. And certainly as that which is termed a moth is attracted to flame, so to everyone of you that bear that living light, attracted to you will be those who are also bruised, to whom the light resonates deep within their soul as something primeval, long-ago forgotten, remembered, almost.

And they, too, will come and need to be loved, feel important, need to be helped. And you, too, will be a light in the darkness who can set other lanterns aflame. And perhaps again two million strong will exist not because they were intimidated by fear or superstition or a malicious God but because of truth, an individual divinity — not one divinity but an individual one; not one God but as many as your numbers are — and be a hope that is not shrouded in mysticism and superstition and in unknown dimensions. And although you walk a razor's edge to get there or through mansions unseen, you are a hope that brings genuineness, an enrichment, to an entity whose flame is lit again, whose ancient wisdom comes alive again in diligent purpose, who finds reason for their life, who finds purpose in loving who they are and seeing it grow like some majestic God, who can change the world — not as tyrants but as flames of truth — into superconsciousness. Hope should never be conjectured.

Yesterday I taught about the nature of reality. For those of you who were here, it will take a year to live every sentence that was taught, for it was a teaching that took one year to learn in the ancient schools and it is a truth that will ring true to you wherever you are. The nature of reality and what you heard yesterday is going to roll on you for one year. Now the difficulty is that some of you are back here the second day! And you're going to hear about the ancient wisdoms and their destruction and how you played a part in that. So now that teaching was the second, third and fourth year of the ancient schools.

I made this comment yesterday, that you live in a fast carry-out civilization, and I feel as if I must "teach and carry!" Well, that school would have taken those many years, that in one day you hear one sentence and the rest of the day is spent creating that sentence through the spiral of time and by the end of the day you would have manifested its knowledge, that you could hold it in front of you. In the ancient schools you learned to do that.

Now in this modern school, you come and sit and you're going to hear, and then you're going to leave here and go back downtown and do all the things you do. So now for those that were here yesterday, we have set a sentence for every day to unfold according to the nature of reality, that that manifested spiral that I set into motion for them is going to happen.

Now here they're back today getting three more years of knowledge, which means that they manifest destiny one sentence a day. And now out of the ancient teachings they get three a day. And by the end of the day they have massive headaches! They find themselves somewhat confused, tattered and torn, and don't know what they did to bring all of this upon themselves! Their memory is so short, they forgot they came to this audience! Yes, they do! And the victims say, "Well, this is my fire. This is my penance. This is what I pay for thinking I'm God." Big deal! Well, you see, you're going to sit here and I'm going to press it to you very condensed, and everything that I'm not saying you will experience and everything that I am saying you will

The Destruction of Ancient Wisdom and Its Resurrection — Morning Session

experience and you will do so for a year. You have to.

Now this is a teaching of three years. So we know at least that all of you here that came yesterday and are here today are going to live for five more years! Yes! Yes, you are! Because, you see, entities who stop learning or are in the groove where they are repeating their lifestyle, their life can be terminated at any frame very easily so it just happens that way. Entities who through the spiral of time have learning they have to do, in the next five years in every creation of reality part of this learning they are creating their reality from. So they cannot leave this place by accident or disease or any other way until they have fulfilled that learning.

Well, now listen you! How come you didn't know that? Where were you yesterday? Yesterday we talked about the nature of reality and that you create that reality according to your consciousness and through the spiral of time, of conscious mind and subconscious mind, through matter and antimatter and the magnetism that is relative to quantum creativity!

So you're scheduled and you're tied up in your appointment book on the spiral for five years! And nothing happens to you that that God within you does not declare so, and this is that God's hour. So for five years you're going to learn. So be it! Yes.

Now that was the nature of reality; see how powerful it is? Yes.

Now in teaching you who are bruised, I brought together these teachings to really resound "Behold God," the Ram's original address, with a lot more "indeed, as it were, in this time as you know it; so be it, indeed; as it were, in this time as you know it; behold God," just to clarify that. Now you come here having all of your boxes rattled.

You've made tremendous changes in your life based on this truth. And you're starting to recognize a divine presence about who you are. So now I don't have to continue to stroke you. You are growing up now to learn some knowledge. That if you'll just listen, that which is the imageless God, you are will come forward and take control because the knowledge supersedes the altered ego. And all you have to do is just listen.

The knowledge flows like a river, clean, bright, pure. And with every dark crevice it fills it up with the waters of life, truth. And as you listen, your consciousness will continue to expand sentence by sentence by sentence and that you are no longer superstitious, fearful, tenuous little creatures but that you are conscious mass on a divine mission. And that there is nothing unreasonable about what you do and how you live your life because you have an understanding. And you're able to think, to open your mind, to heal yourselves, to have pure reason and not be buffooned out of it.

So all I want you to do is listen. And there are some of you in this audience that will phase out on some of these teachings. If I slap my hand, stomp my feet — they're small — it is to wake you up, because you are being phased out by your altered ego; a "beige-ing" is trying to happen. So I'll wake you back up that you listen clearly. All I want you to do is listen, and from that understanding hold it in here, and changes will happen for you. That's all you have to do. For the next few years, the reality from what you heard will create a whole new sandbox for you. So be it.

Creation is not an act; it is a process. There's a difference. Creation is a process; it is not an act. You do not consciously have to create; it is a natural accord of who and what you are.

Now ancient wisdom was always there with every civilization to be supportive of the initiates, to be there, that whatever they created they would not become lost emotionally in that creation, that they could come, liken unto a filling station, and get filled back up with purpose. So oftentimes, since the beginnings of the evolution, in the beauty of the human drama you've gotten lost in the purpose of what you created and why you created it. So the ancient schools were there to remind you of the laws set down in the Book of Life entitled Involution. Involution is the destiny written in the seven levels of the fall of your spirit.

Now ancient wisdom is your birthright and your spiritual cosmology, what you are made up of. Now we have to go back as to who you are, because that was the beginning, to determine your quest and purpose in density of matter called flesh.

And in the ancient wisdoms and the addressing of the nature of reality, it was imperative to talk about what it was that was creating the reality, in particular you. And the ancient wisdoms addressed each entity as being equal unto one another; and they are and you are. Now creation, the natural process, is natural within you. It is needed within you; that is your purpose.

Now let's go back and address what the ancient wisdoms were and why you have bypassed them and caught yourself in an emotional storm called identity.

Now some of you have heard this teaching and some of you heard this teaching and haven't heard this teaching. So we'll have to go back to determine what you are. What you are; not who you are, what you are.

The beginning is a causation. In the beginning we talk about the Is. You have not the mind to contemplate an ongoingness of space, devoid of light, a "just Is." And yet the Is was a sleeping thought that gave premise to the vastness of nothing.

Now the Is is one vast nothing, yet all things materially and potentially. When the Is stirred and contemplated itself, it rolled into within. And at that moment light, the light that filled the void, was created because light is the first creation frequency of thought that has contemplated itself. The Is awakened in a moment and gave birth to conscious light; not life, light.

And the light filled the void and the light was made up of light particum,* like stars. And each light particum was that which is termed the seventh. The seventh light, it is the ultimate, it is the highest frequency there is, light particum. Now we have a stirring intelligence that has been called Spirit. Each light particum was called Spirit and it was also called God.

The Is, the nothing that all things potentially are, is the ultimate giver of life. It is the subconscious mind and from the subconscious mind it contemplated itself, gave birth to consciousness, and consciousness is the light particum and everyone of you are, everyone of you. And in stirring intelligence, it awakened. It awakened from the slumber and became life. Everyone of you make up the light particums because each of you are that. Consciousness, that was light.

Now this consciousness continues to pull from subconscious the Is. It began to stir; stirring is activity. We're not speaking of dead matter! We are speaking of electrified spirit consciousness moving, lights blazing, shimmering, pulsating, intelligence; God.

At the moment the light stirred and was aware of itself, its soul was born. A soul is not God. A soul is an energized record of conscious activity recorded forever. And the moment the soul was given life to by conscious activity, energy was born immediately because when you

---

*Ramtha refers to a light particle as a light particum.

THE ANCIENT SCHOOLS OF WISDOM

begin to contemplate a thought, it broadens consciousness and the action of broadening consciousness is an energy action. Action is energy.

Now they became consciousness and energy, the only two principles of all that is, all that is all. And consciousness and energy created the life force, the principal cause, the mover of action, intelligent action.

Now what are you at this point? You are light, not electric light but light that could fill the void, brilliant. You are intelligence, aware. You have awareness; you are aware of yourself. You are being fed by subconscious mind that is flowing to you, that keeps consciousness aware. And the moment you are aware, you have created the soul to record its awareness. And the moment the soul is created, energy is created. So you make up two principles that are the only principles in a moving universe: consciousness and energy.

Now consciousness. If you only had consciousness, you would have an intelligence that is sleeping; you would have the Is. If you had only energy, you would have a violent reaction to creation. Remember, creation is a process! It is unfolding every moment! It is the natural life! It is the purpose, the process. If you have energy without intelligence, you have violence, the violence to the degree of an exploding nova, of a volcano spewing forth its red-hot fire, vomiting upon the earth. You have the violence of the earth breaking in two, you have the violence of the sun and its storms. That is life set into motion creating. It is not thinking; it is the principal cause creating.

Now the consciousness and energy that constitute you are inextricably combined and every conscious move that you have, it is recorded in the soul as it is created by energy, and those two constitute the nature of reality.

Now hold on here for a moment. You're not this, and you're not this, or what you wear. That's character, that's image, for the sake of experiencing a reality to glean wisdom from for the sake of creation. You are that light particum. You are God. And that energy is what unrolled this universe and all parallel universes.

Now the ancient wisdom that is recorded says that in the light that was created there was a large group of light particum that, feeding on subconscious mind which is the Is, had made a decisive choice. Now listen. And the choice was to take the adventure all the way to its zenith, to discover through the density of what the Is is, of what created reality is, for the full discovery of God. At that moment on the seventh level — there was not the sixth, what you call fifth, fourth, third, second and first; they never existed. It was only light in the void that existed, firing intelligence, that every moment that it stirred it shot off light into the void like a glittering ray, wonderful light that was realization, reality, coming from conscious life. But there were no levels, only the seventh: consciousness and subconscious mind.

And from this group came a selected few who would choose, through the activity of their consciousness, to consume the subconscious mind. You see, God is not glorified in its inception; it is glorified in its consumption. That decision came from consciously expanding entities who made the remarkable journey through all the forms of thought, taking it all the way to its lowest form and back home again. That every level the light grows larger and larger and the subconscious mind is being consumed more and more. And that consciousness that is consuming, it is creating reality from it; it is exploring it; it's recording in its Book of Life the wisdom of creation, creation, a natural process — it is not an act — naturally! For the adventure was to create out of one vast nothing all things materially and potentially.

Now they began to record in their book these adventures of light. On every page they would record the expansion of consciousness, and the election — and painful election that it was — to lower the brilliance of what they were as far as that light could go. And they would call the title of this book, in spirit, the Book of Life, Involution. And in Involution they had seven pages illuminated, in which every page represented a lowered frequency level to the furthermost depths of the mind of the Is they could go. But to make the journey they would need to lower, dim, become slower as to what they were, to make this very dense journey.

So in the Book of Involution a very large amount of pilgrims set sail for the most harrowing, the most painful, the most unknown journey there ever was, the journey of angels to become flesh. Gods, beholden in their splendor, falling — yes, they were — through the seven levels and the glittering with the majesty of their light dimming as they fell to earth. And, behold, the deep moved as the great wind of their being passed over it: So you are.

Seventh, sixth, fifth are indescribable levels. I have no words to tell you what those frequencies were and those journeys, because it is beyond words and it is beyond calculated thinking to say what the journeys were.

But on the fourth level a great separation occurred. And the separation was of those who would go no further and the group that continued to make this journey. And the separation of the Gods happened. And there are those entities that still exist that never became flesh and blood. They are safe. They are the condemners of man and woman. And they don't understand and neither will they know Christ because they have not completed the ultimate journey.

Now on the fourth vibration, on the fourth page in Involution, this is where your bodies come into play — because the fourth was the fourth page — and it was necessary to create the epigenetics. Epigenetics is the pattern of design in genetics that would set the principal cause, or the life force, into cellular mass to reproduce the ideal. You have the marriage of Spirit hovering over mass to create intelligent matter in the processes called "epigenetic process." And on the fourth level everyone of you participated in setting forth the standards of the worlds. Worlds, do you know the term? Planets, rooms, hovered by cloud mass, that the intelligence or the Spirit could move upon mass and create living matter from dead matter, genetics.

Where do you think the pattern in genetics comes from? Where did the single cell get the intelligence to split into two and then into four and to continue the hexagon to create an ideal? Don't you know that one scraping of any cell in your body holds the genetic pattern of the whole of what you are? How do you think cloning is possible? And don't you know that a liver cell knows it's a liver cell? And don't you know that if you inject that liver cell on your earlobe, it will find itself to the liver? Where do you think that intelligence came from?

That intelligence came from page four, the design of epigenetic, alive, mass. In other words, life started moving, conscious life: the animal kingdom, mineral kingdom, plant kingdom, insect kingdom; every kingdom that you can imagine! Creation! Remember, creation is a process. It is a natural, funded consciousness, life. And the body of man and woman would take place on the fourth level design of epigenetics.

Now there's a splitting of the Gods. Already you have grown because you have gone four levels into density; you have lowered that light, that frequency that you are. You keep lowering it and lowering it to every level. And the level is created by the nature of reality. Every level is created as a result of consciousness. And its reality is created by the energy that consciousness directs, because the levels didn't exist before, but they do now! The nature of reality created them.

Then we go to the last three pages. The last three pages are physical, mental, astral, experiencing all three of those. And, behold, the image of man and woman has had the breath of life breathed into it. And man and woman become a living soul, created by spirit, created by God. The breath of life is consciousness and energy and that soul recording every movement.

So you had lifetimes creating reality on the first level.

Now there's a journey and a map in your physical bodies that represent the journey in involution. It has to be there because, you see, the journey is in the soul, and what the soul is it declares the body to be. So all of you have in you the map back home. "I got here, how do I get out of here!" Yes? And that map is the seals in the body. And the seals in the body represent the levels of vibratory frequency that allow the entity to begin the book called Evolution.

Now we're on the back side of the book. The book cover has been turned over in the soul and the new title of this book is called Evolution. And evolution is the exquisite word for creative change. And in order to create change you have to have time, because time is indicative of evolution. And so the spiral of time is created on the densest level there is, the slowest level that there is because spirit no longer is free; it is entrapped in mass, which, if you reverse it all the way back seven vibrations, it too goes back to mind, God, and then Is.

So everything here, everything, is a lowered vibration of a creative thought that occurred on the fourth level. But the creative consciousness on the fourth level created it from subconscious mind and set it into motion.

Now we have a new book; it's called Evolution. And here you have Gods that lit up the void, a conscious stirring, that brought to life the unconscious being. Their duty, their process, if they choose, is to explore the depths of I Am, to create the realities everywhere consciousness walked or thought or emotionally felt. That in the one vast nothing the journey of the Gods would be to create the reality from nothing and make it alive, God to awaken, to know itself, to fill the nothing with life, intelligence, the blooms of creation. That was the courageous yet painful choice of all of you sitting in this audience. Me, too! Count me in your number falling.

Now, people, on page one of Evolution the body that was created epigenetically now is a genetic physical being. And it doesn't look like anything you look like today. It doesn't smell anything like you smell like today. Yet it was innocent. It did not discern beauty because it didn't know ugliness; it only knew life. And the great spirit that filled the void was now a humped-over, hairy, bad-smelling entity experiencing reality and creating things that it never knew before. And it is pressed to create. And the brain size in the cavity of this being is very small. It didn't need a large one. That would come genetically in evolution. But the entity began to evolve through reaction and interaction.

Now this is where you get hung up: consciousness and energy, to create, the process "naturalle" to create, by expanding consciousness to go where you have never gone before, the great unknown. And in that unknown, every step of the way you paint the picture of realization because it doesn't exist unless you go there. And you paint in that picture life forms that genetically take form in light, of trees and flora and fauna that you experience. And everything that you experience, as you walk into the unknown, you're stretching your consciousness. You experience it, you have an emotional feeling from that experience, it is recorded in the book as wisdom and now it exists. And the reality, the nature of your reality, even in those days was growing.

So you create by consciously walking the unknown, abstract, untread thought. Subconscious mind is exactly that; that is the unknown. You dare to pull out of the unknown an unknown thought. You dare to walk a life that is unrealized. And every unknown thought you pull up you experience it in consciousness. The moment consciousness proclaims it, energy creates it. The moment energy creates it, you interact with it. The moment that you interact with it, you have emotional impact. Creation is now realized. It is recorded as wisdom. And then your reality is broadened; now it exists.

And you did that for ten million years. And every life was like a day in this life. And every being that lived and their body died came back again with a spirit and soul enriched, that the next body chosen would genetically match the need to write on the next page. Characters; the body represented characters intentionally created for this journey.

What do you look like all through this? Do you think you looked like you? No! You have looked like a blazing light, a spirit, a ghost, an apparition. That is a divine being; it is the aura around you; it is the spirit that walks in front of you. Your intuitiveness only comes from the God within deciphering the unknown walking before you. And you think you just picked it up!

This being lays down this character; it has recorded in its book. It chooses another who has longer legs and longer arms, bigger brain, to experience the next characterization that will allow the entity to create from subconscious mind reality. It is going home through the back door! You understand? And the subconscious mind is eager to give to the conscious. The God, this great imageless God who has laid down garments of lifetimes, lifetimes, picks up, lives and lays down; eager to continue this journey unknown.

Now there have been civilizations that have gone all the way home before you. There have been entities so engaged, yes, old civilizations, that they interacted with other civilizations in other star systems. And so advanced were they, because they understood consciousness and energy, the principles that created the universe, they had nothing that blocked the communication of their brothers far, far away. There on a thought form, they could send it back and forth. They communicated with one another. There was nothing that kept intergalactic visitations. There was nothing that inhibited the camaraderie of beings, nothing! No superstitions, no blocks, no priorities; only the hunger to create. Joy comes from creation.

There are still some remnants of this evidence that has not completely been destroyed by religion that still exists. There are the great stones on an island that is the remnant of an ancient continent that has all the stones that are looking up to the sky. Don't you know what those are? They happen to be entities just like you, consciousness and energy, evolving here, that had that interaction but one day left here. And the stones they created in a fine cut of light were to be eternally a reminder to you to "Look out there. I'm coming back."

Now there are civilizations that are waiting. There are Gods. They are the same as you, but they don't look like you. But, you see, that was never important. It was never important what color your eyes were, what color your hair was, if you smell good or not. It never was important because there was no altered ego created for the longest time. There was no image and no ideal because everyone was equal. And no matter what the life form looked like, it was still a God and that was undeniable. How can you deny huge, black eyes that when you look at them you feel they love you completely? How can you say that isn't a God? For how can you look into eyes that look like silk blowing in the noonday sun and when they look at you they love you completely? How can you say that isn't a God in those eyes? Doesn't make any difference.

Now evolution is rolling along. And the ancient wisdom reminded us where we came from. My forefathers genetically, in my lifetime, lived underground. They could not live above the ground. They came out at night when there were not that many nocturnal beasts that roamed where we lived. And they had temples in the highest mountain tops where the elders would go and worship by the waxing Enchantress. And they were not technical people, but they were Ancients who knew from whence they came. The elders taught the younger who they were and welcomed them as equals. This ancient wisdom that you're talking about used to, at one time, be inscribed on living rock in our temples. And my people always looked out because they knew from whence they came, and that was all that was important. And they experienced life not in judgment but in creation.

But they're long gone. And the shores of this land that you live on here, do you know why it rains so much here? Not only is it a blessing — never curse the waters from the sky — but the reason it is so holy is because in the last cataclysms the elders remained in their land and sent the likes of me away. And they wept as the latter part of their beloved land went under the waters when the stratum broke. And the weeping was the love of this life, the love of nature. They understood that when you look at a flower you are looking at the principal life cause. And that if you recognize the Is, the principal life cause becomes conscious in this flower. That if you recognize it, a God recognizing a creation, the creation will respond to you. It will talk to you. It will move when you walk by because you have recognized it was alive.

The trees, primeval trees, very few of them exist this day or have been left from the cataclysms, but the trees were living souls; they were beings. Now they were only beings because my people, in the ancient wisdom, understood the living life force of this being. And there were ancient ones and then there were young ones. But my people held them in reverence. Now my people's truth is still remnant in Indians today.

So the rains come here; they are the weeping of ancient Gods. That energy would set itself here for all of time because here, in the

The Destruction of Ancient Wisdom and Its Resurrection — Morning Session

spiral of time, was set about long ago a preservation of the ancient ones and their energy. And these are the shores in which their land was swept under. These are its shores. Now when the rains come, remember they are representative of weeping Gods to never to forget who you are in this truth.

Now the days of old on this earth were so glorious. It was very common for you to sail in a light ship. Except in those days some that were created by civilization could only go in a straight line; they went from point to point. Great lanterns were on the front of these ships; they were wonderful to behold. And they'd start at one triad and go to another one and let off a load and hit another one and let off a load, because they floated on light. Because, you see, the ancients in ancient wisdom understood something that you don't know yet, and that is that earth, like everything in this vibration, is really coagulated thought and that in its coagulation it is really a concentration of wave lengths.

Your earth, if you could see it as magnetic energy, you would see that it looks very much like someone recently described, a ball of twine rolled and rolled and rolled. You know what that is? In my day women made that from the hairs of cattle, great balls, smelly great balls, that everywhere that these threads of energy crossed like this, that in the crossing of those two energy fields matter was created, blurp. So your earth is crossed energy and it's crossed itself so many times you have these blurp-blurps that give off matter, blurp. They give off the constant of density. And as it whirls, it creates a magnetic force and it becomes one powerful generator. Well, the ancients knew how to sail a light ship on the grids of these energy crossings because where they crossed there is no gravity, and the gravity becomes antigravity at that moment. When a wave or a sound is hummed in the area, all that is brought forward in that moment is antigravity and antimatter. And they knew that; it was that simple.

Now these wonderful civilizations that came and went did wondrous things and not once did they have superstition involved. And every new civilization that started all over again went all through the basics, through the humped-over hairy stage of evolving, very rapidly.

The schools were just there — they were everywhere — to come in and remember, "You're creating this. This pain is now an illusion. You have already gained the experience. Absolve the experience and the pain will go away! Rise your energy up! Think about this!"

They would bring entities in and lay them on slabs under great pyramids, and the shaft of light would open and they would lay there. And the great, great beings would say to them, "This is the experience you gained. This is what you created in consciousness. This is your reality. You are now stuck in this reality because you emotionally are in a storm that does not allow you to rise above it consciously and take the illusion away." So they would do that, and the cripples would get up and walk out. Very simple. All a matter of consciousness and energy.

Now with the ancient wisdoms it was not uncommon for beings from great distances to come and to share energy. Your great Ra-Ta-Bin triad (pyramid), if you will notice, it is dedicated to the chariots beyond the sun. Great peoples had come from the other side of your sun and their interaction here taught many a lot. And many have left this place and live there now. And some of those have intermingled and interbred and are here. That was their choice for their soul's evolution.

Now you're sitting here and you are endeavoring to relate to this and there are things going on inside. Something is saying, "Yeah, yeah, yeah! You know that! Wake up! This is truth." And there is a part of you that is the bruiser that says, "Come on! Come on! This is incredulous stuff!" Can you think of a better story of your creation, eh? This is creation and it is truth, and the "Come on, give me a break now" is the bruiser who's riddled in superstition.

How does this affect who are you now? It has everything to do with who you are now because in a few more years you won't be who you are now. You just won't, because too much knowledge has a way of burning away the image. It does. Ask me; it does!

Now the image stays in place because of ignorance and superstition. Now you — yes, you — are Gods of light on a destiny of creation. And who you are is struggling to break away from an image, that you can continue the journey of light.

How are you going to go to the other side of this sun until you understand why you can't? How are you going to be happy? How are you going to love who you are? How are you going to create and justify it until you understand why? How can you accept nature with utter grace until you have knowledge?

Your bruised, superstitious, stuck, repetitive self, that has deleted you from the cosmic journey of big business is what has caused your

The Destruction of Ancient Wisdom and Its Resurrection — Morning Session

stagnation in this lifetime, caused you to want to take your life in this lifetime, has caused you to ruin your brain with alcohol and drugs. It has caused you to be a tyrant and an enslaver. It has caused you to prostitute yourself for the sake of the image and acceptance. It has caused you to suppress the truth and speak falsehoods, bearing false witnesses and to live as the hypocrite. It has been that which has taken part of the truth and sensationalized it and created fear and mockery. It is that which has taken the pure essence of what God is and turned it into an insecure, self-conscious, psychotic being. It is that essence that removes the quality of divinity from yourself and others around you, that you can control them or make them your equal: losers in life.

It is that essence that blinds you to the eternal movement of creation, that blinds you to the necessity of evolution. It is that essence that stagnates you in change and causes you to be so afraid. You urinate in your breeches to think you have to make a decision on your own! It is the essence that inhibits you from reasoning because you are stuck in fear because you don't know how to think for yourself because you never try. You're afraid to be alone because of what you would find out about you. You're afraid to give your opinion and your truth because you think you'll be wrong. And you don't even try because you're afraid you'll fail.

Images are that which is termed the betrayer to who you are inside. They are terrified to evolve beyond what is socially acceptable. There is no basis; everything you do is on someone else's advice. They are the ultimate victim, that if it goes wrong they'll have someone to blame.

It pains me to see you be so afraid that you're going to lose this life. You never lived it! You never rode in a light ship. You never went beyond the sun. You never just went into a place and laid down and allowed a shaft of light to come upon you and there is a hum in the background, and in that moment you realize that in your creation that you created being stuck there. And the physical disability leaves you the moment you realize it. For some of you can't fathom Spirit because your whole world is mass. What a pity. And you hold on so desperately to that mass. And you're afraid to die, and every day it approaches.

The Spirit, the ancient wisdom, is that you're God; not the image. That what is within you that waits so patiently for you to turn this page, this imageless being that allows you to create the characterization, the bruiser, the destroyer, awaits for consciousness and that splendor of a moment to call it forth, to burn it away. "I want to know." It takes courage to say, "Who am I?" And it takes greater courage to hear a knowledge and be willing to live it because these few moments of life are only a few moments in the light of all eternity on those levels, those wonderful levels that stay stationary through involution, where there is no time; there's only forever.

What happened? Why are you so stuck in this image? Why is it so important to you to hold onto youth? Why is it so important for you to think that you're a man because you have a penis and semen, or to think you're a woman because you have a breast and womb? What is it about you that needs so desperately to declare your sexuality or your preference? What is it about you that has destroyed your life and any hope for joy? Because you don't feel worthy of it. Why? Why don't you know you are God? Not saying the word, being the word, with fire coming from those eyes and joy emanating from that being.

Seven and a half million years ago a very insecure person, man, took away from women the right to be God, and they all went along with the game. It was an experience, you must understand. And these people were going to school to understand that you create reality from subconscious mind by being conscious, that you create consciously and your energy creates; whatever you think manifests and that creates reality. And these schools were there to tell you you created this experience that you may gain this wisdom and now you will own it; it becomes a reality, but you will never have to engage it again. And now you can go to the next adventure.

And every moment you are turning those pages. And the energy that was sitting here at the base level begins to travel up through here and the entity becomes illuminated. You only gain illumination in the fourth. The rest of it is the journey to get there. It is all pain, powerful pain. It still is in this audience!

So every experience is raising the energy because, remember, creation is a process. It is not an act; it is natural. Consciousness and energy is God. The Is is the subconscious mind which consciousness consumes to make known reality, to go there and be healed, so that you don't get stuck, so that you can move on. If you have a little identity problem, you go to the school. Your school may last a year.

And you say, "How did the people live?" There was no money in those days; there was only mind that could raise blocks as high as you wanted them and to cut from living rock with light and move them and build. There were fertile lands that people moved upon and took a living seed. Remember the tree, the living soul? The seed was the hope. And they held them in their hands and put them in the ground and they bore fruit straightaway! And they lived and went to school. And when they came out of the study, they were no longer caught in the identity but they were progressing on.

Now women, this was a natural creation. And the gist and the "bottom line" was that the subconscious mind would no longer be the conscious mind in women. This was just an experiment, and the experiment was that all the power of subconscious mind would flow to the consciousness of men. It was a definite separation of power that occurred seven and a half million years ago, definite. And we have an unequal balance of power occurring here.

Now listen! Reality; what creates reality? Tell me. *(Consciousness and energy.)* The reality of inequality would have been created by whose consciousness? Yes, both. Now if you create everything else and reality constitutes where your consciousness is, doesn't it also hold that if you say yes, then the reality would occur that women no longer would grow? Are you with me?

And all they had to do was cease it and their consciousness stayed the same. And their energy fell and stayed right here (the reproductive organs) because that was all it was used for. They were denied the right to have a soul, and so they were no longer divine and they were herded like cattle — a new experience — to be propagated upon by men. Men, in turn, lost their feminine quality and stood alone as the sole voice of God and treated their women abusively. And whatever a man declared, so said God was law.

And laws started, you know, in a paradise that had borne fruit from a tree of knowledge. It had created Edens untold; angels had walked there and Gods had walked there. Communication, intelligence, love and light — truly, not words of the New Age, but words of primeval that meant something that were the actions of reality.

And the curtain came down.

Who was this person? God? Yes. And the person was an entity who in consciousness began to lose touch and did not go to the schools, got caught in the dream, and the dream was the need to be recognized. Tyrants are born from the reality of the lack of recognition and they start as followers. And they need to be loved, stroked and adored. And every interaction with that experience they go onto the wheel. And with more interaction, the lack grows larger and larger and larger and the tyrant who starts with one ends up with a multitude. What happens? In your dream, in your image, when you need to be recognized, it's called jealousy.

This person got caught in the dream and ceased to grow and therefore the energy had not moved to this wonderful place, page four in the Book of Life. Hopefully, you're on it, but his had not gone there; it had stayed here in the third seal called power. And in that powerful place there is no creation happening, only stagnation. And yet the God inside is saying, "Move! Move! You have to do something!"

Don't you know where anxiety comes from? Anxiety comes from the lack of creation. And stress comes from creating someone else, not yourself.

This entity was then hungry for the great lack. His God inside was saying, "Move, move out of this place. We owned this." It's the voice inside. It's the voice of the wilderness crying out. And this person said, "God is speaking to me." And instead of moving that energy and expanding that consciousness to resolve the dilemma, the entity stayed in the same consciousness, listening to this voice and decreed it so! And thus began the fall of women, who suffer even this day in that image, and men and the creation of the supreme altered ego that is ruled by copulation and pain. And those are fantasies that work together, and those in turn are ruled in power in subjugation.

And man got caught. And his whole image, for seven and a half million years, began to solidify in every lifetime. No longer was he able to lay down and pick up the bodies objectively. He now became a subjective being who would pick up a body and repeat. He ceased the spiral and created the circle, the rut. And no matter how many bodies he laid down and picked up, he was the same image because now, with this glorious light that passes from birth to death and in between, this consciousness and energy carried a film with it, a layer. It was a personality taking form, an image taking form, that was definite and distinctive. And every body it picked up, every experience repeated itself, which solidified and held the energy that man could not evolve here to become that great being that creation and consciousness and energy demanded him to. He denied himself a journey and he's still treading on the wheel.

Why can't he cry and love? Why can't he be compassionate? Barbarians can be compassionate! A warrior can love and be merciful and have grace! But that is when a barbarian is changing, moving through the layers, turning the pages in search of self, God. Men do not move here. Some move to go past it but at great cost. It's very painful, this journey, because what keeps the altered-ego image is the adoration, not of women but of men to another man.

And remember you only attract to you the reality that you're equal to. You cannot have another one in your life if that person does not reflect who you are. And men have a powerful desire to congregate with men. And everyone's image reflects to one another, and there all realities are the same size. And if anyone moves out of it — well, you know what that ridicule's all about — so the block is built up here.

And women? Well, women are servicing. They're bitching and whoring and bringing children forth in unbelievable numbers. They're getting more competitive because their whole life is based on beauty. And so every lifetime their survival is locked into their physical reality and they're not moving beyond it.

So what do we have now? Women struggling with their identity. And people look at them and say, "Well, you're a woman, don't you know that? Look at you. You have all this equipment; you're a woman. What else do you want?"

"No. I am more than a woman and I do not need your permission to be it." Woman knew. Women knew!

And a man who looks at his peers and says, "I shall not curse, for the filth will not roll off my tongue that degrades life. To make an abomination out of my penis and a woman's vagina, to call copulation a filthy word, to talk about human feces and urine and criticizing it." Don't you know that one who utilizes such terms are those who are living and fighting in these levels? You are what you speak. And the man says, "No." It takes a great man to turn and walk away, to show grace and mercy and humility.

Know you why religion drew so many men long ago? Because in their soul God had elected them to ratify what he was. And don't you know that men also had an innate, ancient desire to move beyond their image, to know what it is to be merciful, filled with grace and have compassion?

Now this man introduced this form. Then there would come many,

THE ANCIENT SCHOOLS OF WISDOM

many centuries later more men — no women, only men — who would introduce more and more, and slowly you began to see the decay of the ancient schools. There were no women coming, unless they had shaved their heads and bound their breasts and calloused their hands that they may appear as men, that they can go through and become an initiate. And some for the painful desire of leaving this place.

And then comes another man who introduces superstition, the destroyer and the cementer of the image. That image that won't leave you alone lifetime after lifetime after lifetime. Superstition; what is that? They took from the ancient schools this truth — now listen carefully and if it sounds familiar, you are awakening:

That "God is terrible. God punishes us. He condemns us if we have not followed his law and his doctrine. So say I. The volcano that erupted was the wrath of God upon his people. Violence, anger, death, pestilence is God punishing you, his children. Why? Because you are ruled by an evil force and that evil force was kicked out of heaven and took all his angels with him, the fallen Gods. And wicked were they. And all of this earth was given as their dominion. They are the demons and devils and they are ruled by one leader. The temptations of the flesh are from these fallen ones that were kicked out of heaven and fell to this earth, and they rule this earth. You have to abide by these things. You cannot sin! You cannot question! God demands that you be saved, for you have sinned and you have listened to the tempter. God, who has given you a chance, wants you to be saved. For this God is powerful. He flung the yellow sun into its orbit. He can shatter the earth. He created it in seven days!

"And God is waiting for you to worship him, to listen to him."

Now God created the earth and the heavens in seven days: It was seven levels of vibration in mass that created the heavens and the earth, the firmament. Everything that is mass is coagulated vibration; it's vibrating all at the same level. And it is a thought conceived in the mind of consciousness that was lowered every step to become living matter, the life force. And in seven levels it was conceived, not in seven days. Do you understand where it came from? Snatch a little bit of truth here.

Now, "And the Gods were kicked out of heaven and they were fallen spirits. And their rule would be this dominion and this mass." What does that sound like? Yes, the fallen Gods are all of you, including the preacher, because all who elected to take this journey did so, and it was called the great fall of the Gods, the Spirit that moved. What Spirit do you think moved across the face of the deep? It came like a great wind and it was all of you. The "fallen spirits" were the ancient wisdom of each individual and who they were on this journey. And those Gods had no mystery at all about them, that their rule was to go through mass. And their sin was that they were of matter. Yes! Because matter to become intelligence is controlled by consciousness, Spirit. Dead matter is given life through intelligence and they're saved.

Don't you know in the book within the soul, called Evolution, that the path back home, back from whence you came in this journey, is to come out of this painful expression with joy. Being saved does not mean that you're helpless; it means that you have a necessity to finish this expression, that you can go home and not be locked in matter for eternity! That's what it meant in the ancient schools.

In the seventh year of the ancient teachings it talked about the journey in the last days of the singular garment and that it had overcome, that it had persevered, that it was diligent, that along the way it had created divinity. Divinity had not created it! It created divinity and had become the moral and spiritual qualifier of all life that it had created in its realities.

And the Christ — yes, yes, the son of God — there will be the daughters of God, who in the last days in this journey are not saved; they will have conquered themselves. They have consumed — yes, the glory is not in the inception of creation, it is in its consumption — and they have consumed and have owned it all. And behold the void is afire with light because what was unconscious shimmers in consciousness, for all things are eternal in this kingdom.

Superstitious people, insecure, locked-into-energy people, too-image people, create and take from ancient truths and break it up and create their own religions. They take the cosmology of a simple truth and make it into a superstition, taking God out of the entity, putting him "up there," making him insecure in that you have to worship him. Why would "little ol' you" need to glorify "big ol' that?" Get it?

And if "big ol' that" was eternal, that in the palm of its hand — his — that the past, present and future existed simultaneously, that in the Garden of Eden when he dared to pick from the tree according to the serpent — and the serpent represented wisdom; that's what it meant in cosmology — dared to take the apple off of the tree, intending poor, ignorant Adam to get off of his rear end and start living and that God was shocked and appalled that they would do this in his place, now I ask you: This eternal being, who knew past, present, and future, knew it all, didn't he plan this whole scheme? And then why did he have to pretend he was so shocked?

Well, you see, they don't understand because they have not evolved, to continue to create, to gain knowledge. They put the damper on that and said, "Never question. It is the word of God. And you do not want to have that wrath put upon you. Never question. Stay right here." That comes from entities who are tyrants, who started out just wanting to be acknowledged and got stuck and could go no farther and created a sandbox of enormous persuasion.

Now that superstitious man has since separated nations and boundaries and peoples, and war upon war upon war has ensued over religious dogma. Blood has been spattered, children have been slaughtered, women have had their eyes poked out with hot irons, and hideous books were put together upon the selection of only one people, instead of all peoples, branding the black man as evil, in the name of God.

In all of the ancient schools this truth came in fragments. And because they didn't understand, they took it and reorganized it and rewrote it and created an enslavement that affixed a characterization that is with you this day, that bruises you every time you try to change. You are conditioned not to.

Now know you that the great teachers fled to high places and others left this plane until the times of change could come back? There are ancient teachers that are still alive; they are thirty thousand-years old. Who do you think are the entities in the light ships? Do you think they live for a hundred years? No. They are beings that have evolved to the seventh, who are perpetual-eternal. Same as you.

Now Buddhism; Buddha was born of a virgin — an immaculate conception — and royal heritage, and he lives many thousands of years prior to Yeshua ben Joseph. Yeshua ben Joseph would come along many thousands of years later. Mohammed was an immaculate conception, born of a virgin. Vishnu, an ancestor of mine, was born of a virgin. Yeshua ben Joseph was born of a virgin. Christianity, religion and all of their myths go all the way back to the teachings of ancient wisdom that said that every God was born in the purity of Spirit, which later they would turn around and say, "All great messiahs were born of virgins," a misinterpretation of the purity of Spirit.

It was imperative, once this was on a roll, to begin to destroy all evidence of these schools and all living records, and they went about for thousands of years destroying. And in the last two thousand, the bloodiest onslaught of warring religion has gone on. And in between there has been no interaction from the people beyond the sun.

The minds have stopped growing; creating has ceased to happen. Intimidation is going on and the image is growing thicker and thicker and thicker. And every experience, over and over and over again, suppresses women to be breeding animals without a mind and a conception of God. And men are to uphold the laws of God and they are divinely chosen and their rewards and booty are the things of this earth! Twenty million people perished in the holy wars.

Ever hear the word sect? Sect meant the ancients running and hiding and still having their schools in secret, the secret schools of the initiates. And "sect" was the name that was given to them! And they were all hunted down! And all of their wonderful temples were destroyed and their people slaughtered. And all initiates that partook were hunted down and slaughtered and their children mutilated in front of them just to uphold a superstitious mind that could not evolve because it needed to have some strokes! And God became a vengeful, warring, mean, son-of-a-bitch. The last schools that were destroyed — their thread of ancient wisdom, only a thread, ran through their ritual — were the Druids.

You have great people who live in the mountains of my home that grow bigger and bigger every day. And they live so far up on the precepts, they live in bitter cold. And they have very little wood to heat them but it has pressed them into growing to the point that they, in consciousness, can create heat all around them and walk around with merely a loin cloth on when the temperatures have plunged way below zero in your time and counting. They have very few things of this world, but they are committed to a remnant of ancient truth. But they have hidden away rather than lived — which is their travesty because, in thinking that, they are continuing with this journey — and they can do things that do marvel self. They are hidden away from the world and they cannot create in the world, because their very lives are threatened by religion. Other than they, all of the people have gone.

And only a religious God exists and his son and his holy ghost. And there's only one way and there's only one word that is very distorted; the word is a compiling of stolen truths of ancient wisdom that for one who was not qualified to understand the living word, religion has interpreted it according to their perception and made God as violent as a volcano and as threatening as the ending of the world; that the earth is not to live on but to be denied; that to experience life is a sin; to squelch a reasoning mind is a divine stroke of God. And everyone is dying and their lights and those lanterns are turned over and the hot oil is spilling on the earth, one by one.

And what now lives in the place is an image. You know the image? The body looks a certain way. You spent all morning painting your face, trimming your beard, filling in your pockmarks, cutting your hair, oiling your body, dressing in fine silks, fine broadcloth, doing the right thing, saying the right thing. Everyone talks alike. Everyone dresses alike. Everyone goes to the right places. Everyone is high-tech. And here everyone watches the telly or listens to the waves. And all along it's telling them, "Be accepted. Don't be old and lousy! Be new and improved!"

And the voice that cries out in the wilderness is quickly extinguished. It is humiliated and degraded in all public markets. No one is to be above their station in life. It is a society whose lights have gone out and the fanatical religions are on the march to save their souls.

And you go from one fanatical death to another because if you accept the teaching that you are dead in Christ and that if you do not obey these laws, you will go to hell and burn forever.

In the nature of reality, when you know you are a sinner — because this God within says, "Turn the page! This isn't right! Stop condemning your neighbor! It's all right to love someone else!" — when your God within is saying to you, "Turn it off and think! Listen to me! I am the voice in the wilderness! I AM! Meet me in the garden within yourself" — and they tell you, "You can't listen to that, that is the devil speaking to you, the fallen one. He's after you," and you're wavering, you look at your life and it's so empty. No matter how much you get, it's so empty. You look at your life and you're so poor and have so much poverty. You're still empty.

If your consciousness accepts your eternal damnation, your reality will create it and you'll live it; that's part of the wheel. And if your consciousness accepts that this identity, this body — how you look,

The Destruction of Ancient Wisdom and Its Resurrection — Morning Session

where you go — is all there is, you will die in the grave and you will go back to sleep and the light will go out because you have collapsed consciousness. Remember, you create what you think; it becomes your reality.

Do you know that there is a level of vibration just above this one that there are millions of people lying parallel to the ground asleep waiting to be resurrected? And they haven't gone into another lifetime. And they are jarred to wake up and pleaded to wake up. And since their awakeners do not look like the image of Yeshua ben Joseph, they will not wake up. And the image was someone's painting.

Now listen you! You have bruised yourselves. You have been your own whipping post to consciousness. You have loved spiritual truth as long as it did not have a commitment to it and so long as you could work it in your daily routine. The truth is — and you listen — that the path back home is glorious! It is filled with it! There is no light like the one that is on the next page. There is no such thing as freedom perceived now until it is actually lived.

I conquered myself to be my own law because I knew that there was a destiny for the human being that was far greater than the grave and dying under a noonday sun! Where does the Spirit go? You can't have this brilliant intelligence walking around and not have a purpose for it. Where's it moving to? Does it move the universe or does the universe move it?

The ancient wisdom is that creation is a process, not an act. And it is a natural action and need to every human being whose flickering lamp is still on. And underneath this image, this jealous, insecure, fearful image, lies a brilliant, illuminated being that's just waiting to get on with it, to take you into an adventure of the mind, to allow you to contact and be a part of an intelligence that is equal to who you are.

Remember this! If you haven't had an interaction it is because you don't deserve one, because you are not, to the degree of your reality, equal to attract to you the likeness of what you are! In order to have the people from the other side of the sun make contact, you've got to be worthy of it. And you earn that right by getting on with being who you are: simply, powerfully, beautifully truth, and creating not because you have to because it's a need! You don't have to sit on the floor and think of something; it will flow like a river to you. It presses to you.

And this illuminated being here burns away the image with knowledge. Knowledge is what unlocks the chain and opens the door. It is that knowledge of evolution of the Book of Life.

And God, does he love you? Does she love you? Yes! You wouldn't be here if you were not loved! Love is the grace that allows existence! Yes, you are loved! You have something in you that loves you, that your blood runs hot with its passion. Not a sterile image but something virile and alive, electric and powerful, that when it moves into a room it can light the whole room up. Why do you think you wait for me? What do I have that you love? A reflection of what you are, getting ready to be born; that's what. So be it.

And Spirit, I am Spirit. I am the glory of the God that I Am, that had burned away the Ram. It is a transfiguration that occurs. With St. Francis, it occurred in one moment of contemplation. Without superstition, cutting through, it happens in a moment, the beginning of the journey.

This audience is here to shine onto you what you are. There is no hell and damnation waiting for you! And the greatest punishment you could ever give yourself is not changing. The greatest punishment you could ever inflict, as far as pain, would be to deny what you are inside.

There's a lot going to happen in this place of large, very large, proportions; that's its destiny in the time flow. It's natural. The earth has to change. Everything alive has to change. Everything must have its moments of metamorphosis. And where your home is is no different.

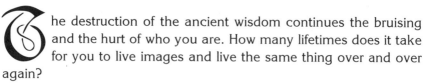

The destruction of the ancient wisdom continues the bruising and the hurt of who you are. How many lifetimes does it take for you to live images and live the same thing over and over again?

There are women in this audience who still think that they can survive by selling their bodies or marrying someone who's going to take care of them. They are still paid-for people; they're soulless. They're afraid to think for themselves. There are men in this audience who still think it's important for a man to spill his seed every single day. And he has created that bodily reaction through his consciousness and holding up his image. There are entities in this audience who still cannot perceive there is something wonderful inside of them. They have a feeling and then they roll it away because, you know, they need the recognition. And they want to find someone that would give it to them because they don't have it in themselves for themselves.

The Destruction of Ancient Wisdom and Its Resurrection — Morning Session

The great pyramids around the world — some are under the ocean — they were ancient temples. They were not a tomb. They were a temple for the living, not the dead. And on their walls in living rock is engraved parts of the ancient wisdom. They are lined up on the magnetic threads of the earth. They are living reminders also of the triad, with their three sides representing astral, physical, mental. And that when you move the energy up through these seals — astral meaning Spirit, mental meaning conscious design, and physical meaning manifestation — when you bring all of them together, you create the fourth energy here.

And the pyramid means "fire in the middle," fiery form. They're aligned on the earth's magnetic fields. Remember, the earth is coagulated threads of energy and these sit right on the blurps. These tombs are five-sided and, when you are within them, knowing what you know, it creates the energies of the sixth and the seventh. They are reminders today of the invisible God within you and they are ancient.

Those are the only visible temples left of the ancient schools.

When you deny yourself or try to intellectualize consciousness and energy, you lose it. When you look, simply see that you are a conscious being consuming the glory of life of the subconscious mind, which all of you possess, by the way. And that creation, to create with your energy the nature of reality, is the process and the journey, that you're in the last throes of the path back home.

When you can look at yourself and your life and say, "I am unhappy because I made myself that way. I did not step aside and look at it and say, 'What have I learned from this?' And the moment that I look at my problems, I have created a more expansive consciousness and higher consciousness. The moment that I do that, the problems resolve in the Book of Life as wisdom and it gives me up. That everything in my life is a result of my attitude. That my life is all options. And what it is, I have made it so. And if I am miserable, I have made myself miserable because I have not had the will, desire or capacity to engage my misery, to turn it into wisdom because I wasn't humble enough to. And if I think my whole life evolves around money, then I am bought and paid for and I'll die as a pauper. That's my reality."

And if your reality is that you're a victim, then you'll never own the wisdom and your consciousness will collapse in on you because you create it. Everything is created by your perception. Everything exists because you perceive it so.

And how do you get happy? You don't have to be saved! You just have to start living. Living! Say, "What do I want?" In the unknown mind, the subconscious mind, the unknown says "Why is it in me to be afraid? Because I have been conditioned to be afraid, to not think for myself or make a decision for myself. And therefore the unknown I have no control over and no one wrote about it and there's no laws about it. And if I go out there I would lose everything!" Don't you know that often in a moment of death, awakening occurs? You can never destroy the consciousness that created the kingdom!

Well, powerful entities that you are, the unknown, remember, is the consuming potential of a consciousness. It is in the unknown mind that antimatter exists. That in the time flow that you create in consciousness, matter is given from antimatter, that consciousness comes from subconsciousness, that all things you could possibly want lie in the one vast nothing that is all things potentially. And the only fearful thing that lies in the unknown is the fear you carry with you when you take the first step. That's all.

Now, pilgrims, all these things are written in your book called Involution. They are ancient truths. They got lost along the way because someone got insecure. All the miracles are not myths; they are the realities of an advanced being.

Own all your superstition. And because you're going to have a little trouble manifesting superstition — remember, you're afraid of it — I'll do it for you! Every superstitious thing you empower, I'll bring it forth, unveil it in your reality and in the moment it appears, it's going to make you frightened. Look right at it and call forth that great God and say, "Come forth!" And the God will say, "Behold, we have gained from this experience. It is no more. So be it." And it will give you up and in the soul will come a wind that is a freeing space.

And fear; what are you afraid of when you get your land? What are you afraid of in these times that are coming? Are you afraid you're going to lose your life? You will never lose who you are. You are eternal. You have a destiny to complete. You have to discover and make light all that is unknown. "Behold, God" is the task that does this.

Some people cannot exist without their superstition. And they've got to have a pretty mean God because they've created that God to keep them in line; that's the game they play. So they can go and do a lot of things, but they can go and ask God to forgive them and that

THE DESTRUCTION OF ANCIENT WISDOM AND ITS RESURRECTION — MORNING SESSION

gives them the permission to say it's okay. Do you understand? And then they just go about doing some more, and then they go in and say, "Forgive me," and it's all done. Do you understand? It's in here.

Now my last runner for you this morning is for you to see your light, your Spirit, this bold and beautiful thing that I see when I look at you. It's not this or that; it is the light, that God that you are, that wonderful adventurer that can walk way out there and bring news back to you way in here. It is that defier of time, distance and space. It is the magician. And you're going to have your morning to see it. So be it.

All you had to do is sit and listen. All you had to was sit and listen.

When you leave this day you'll be much more enlightened than when you came. And the years that are to come from this teaching are the years of ripening not just the word, but what it is to be it. It doesn't matter who you were before this life; you're still the same entity — not the same character but the same entity. It didn't matter what you did before this lifetime. It matters what you're doing now.

These ancient teachings had no dogma that went along with them. There were no amulets that you had to wear or zircons. There were no rituals that you had to do. There is no higher self. That only exists in the groove because consciously if you are endeavoring to achieve the higher self, it means you are the lower self and you will hold yourself a parallel distance from that and you'll never achieve. That's how you create reality. There's no thing you have to do because creation is the natural essence of what you are.

And it's not a discipline either; disciplines belong in the groove. If you have to be God, you aren't God; you're the image. If you have to love, you don't love. If you have to forgive, you never will forgive because you never will forget.

You don't have to move; it's where you are. You don't have to change; you have got to want to. You don't have to be intellectual. Be simple. That is where the glory of God is: consciousness and energy create reality. That's it!

"Boogymen," devils, demons, demigods, higher orders, lower orders, all exist in creative realities. They are phantoms that are someone's insecurity.

In the ancient schools you came and you listened. And for the rest of that day you lived that which you heard and it permeated everything. You just have to listen; it's knowledge. It will light up all those dark corners in your soul. It will do away with your illusions of fear and terror. It will unmask the dark riders and bring you truth. You just have to listen. And that you did very well this long, long morning.

Now if you go and breathe some of this prana, it will heal your body. And look up at the sky that is painted with moving colors and recognize it. Recognize the hunger in your body and bless your food and let it restore you. It's so natural. And give yourself moments that you can get the world off your shoulder and create a reality that is joy and enlightenment by choice. And when you return, I have a wee bit more to say to this audience and perhaps you'll be ready then to hear a little more.

Ancient wisdoms and their destruction, what it means is a bruised soul. Perhaps this day a lot of lanterns were lit. So be it. I love you.

THE DESTRUCTION OF ANCIENT WISDOM AND ITS RESURRECTION

 AFTERNOON SESSION

Indeed! You have learned? Yes. I love you! Let's have a drink, more substance.

To my forever.
It is filled with adventure!
So be it!

You have rested and are filled? You know that when you consume food that your brain puts out chemicals that make you tired. You know that, eh? So you're a little hazy, sleepy.

Tell me, in just sitting and listening and being, did you learn? And what about those images that began to flash before your eyes of incidences in your life of people, places and things, did they happen? At every teaching did something remind you of something? Yes? You're learning, yes.

Now do you understand a little bit more about how things got so messed up? You know you are the only collective civilization, in the pattern of lifetimes that all of you have lived, that are spinning your wheels in the wilderness! Not for forty years but millennias! Going round and round and round and round. And you have brethren and sistren that have long ago made their trek through this density and have returned as brilliant light. So is your destiny. We've just got to get you to realize who you are and what you're dealing with, what is important. So we have made some inroads and in that I am pleased. So be it.

Can you fathom yourself as a Spirit? But it's difficult to think that, when you're so physical and all of the problems that go on in the real world; yes?

I have to tell you, there have been a host that have gone so far with the Ram's ramblings for a long time in your time — it's been going on for ten years, which is what you call a decade; it is just a moment — but they've gone so far and they went so far. When the goodies stopped coming and flowing from me to them and I said, "Now it's time for you to grow up and do it yourself and you have to change to do that," a whole host of them, just like on the fourth level, couldn't go forward with it.

Now are they wrong? No, they're not wrong. And are they right? No, they're not right! It's just that, you understand, where you're living in this sort of society that you live in, the law is that — you know you have to have laws to make laws. Is that not a duality? — you have a social order that's very stringently controlled. Your comings and goings are very much known by people who sit in the places of power.

Now part of this host said, "I'm not going to go back and live on the land and be some barbarian and give up electricity and all the technology that we've gained in 2,000 years. I can't go and change and be sovereign when sovereignty is all around me. I don't have to grow my own food; I simply go and buy it and someone cooks it for me. I give them the money that I work for. I live in a mountain that's got holes in it and I feel safe, even with all the locks on my doors. And the Ram has asked me to go back and live like he, a barbarian, lived."

There is a lot in what these people have said that is truth. But even though my times were arduous indeed, people were free in my time. And civilization, a civilized order, is so constricted and the individual's freedoms do not exist here. Where can you go and be homeless that you're not despised? And what is thought of beggars here? They are a humiliation to the social order. And what about the person who just wants to grow their own food? They are taxed heavily on it, so they can't even live off their own land.

You have it much more denser and have much more of a collapsed consciousness, social consciousness, than were the days and the glory of the Ram and the great march. There are no marches anymore. You cannot go through the great mountains on a trek and cross streams and great bodies of land and walk as free man/free woman! You cannot start a fire unless you have paid someone for a license to do so.

Your social order has created a beige civilization. Christianity has created the dark ages — and they say they are a light to the world. And in the dark times pure reason is despised. An individual is obliterated unless they fit the image of idolization from the masses. Who, like in the days of all the Caesars, Suetonius' twelve Caesars, had to have circuses to be entertained all the time and pacified. You have it much more difficult than I did. I would have rather taken a broadsword in the back than face the thought of having the inability to think for myself. And perhaps this entity was the original libertarian. Perhaps.

She was correct. They are correct. I ask too much. The knowledge is too much. It is so difficult to give up the image in this order. It is so difficult to become white when everyone is beige.

And you can't be free. No, you are not a democracy. You are a socialist government because you're not free people. Freedom has everything to do with what is within you. The danger is the animal that is locked up, that the explosiveness of their energy is primeval and barbaric; they're the dangerous ones. And they're the ones that rule the world.

But I must say this to you: the lanterns that are wavering in the wind, that there is coming a time that is already moving like a wind on the water, that the natural order goes through its phase, its movement, its change, its metamorphosis from the caterpillar into the butterfly. It has been in its chrysalis and it is now breaking through. That is the primeval order called the life force, intelligent matter programmed to change.

No one in a beige society — because they have been so hypnotized that their lanterns have gone out and it's only a dead, living dead, character that communicates back and forth — would have heard and responded to this truth had it not been the right time in the time flow. And the right time is that there is a lot to be said about the times of the Ram and those people, ever-moving and ever-changing, knowing when to make camp and when to break it, knowing when to put into a harvest and when to harvest it. Acutely aware people; you know? That's who you are.

Well, this message of sovereignty, for the sake of God within and that appointment you have with the next five years in counting, is an appointment with destiny, that it is imperative for the diligence of spirit of who you are to have enough knowledge to burn away the image that would rather die than move. Because along with the movement of light principle coming out of this chrysalis, there must be the intelligence that was once the wind on the water, on the deep, the thunder in the firmament, that has to give reason for reality, and that's you. Ancient wisdom.

To survive and to live in harmony doesn't mean that I want you to squat on the land to pass your dung. It doesn't mean that I want you to smell bad because that's what you think you have to do. This is not "have to." This is moving with great intelligence into securing one's place in the time flow until you have accomplished every page in this book. That's destiny; that's real destiny. Not being the doctor or the lawgiver, not meeting Mr. Right or Mrs. Wonderful. Destiny is to evolve during these times, the densest of all times.

I haven't said anything that is really shocking because you're insensitive to shock. You've been decadent. You have lived completely in mass; that is your whole reality. You have been ignorant; you have been the identity. And you have faced death ten thousand times, millions of times. But to the character it's always the greatest fear. But I haven't said anything shocking. I've said things that are true.

In last two thousand years — the first almost fifteen hundred years so many of you in this room lived through — the one "true faith" took hold. There were crusades against the Turks, the ancient Persians and the crusades against the Britons, peoples of the north, for the one true faith. And in every century the snatches of truth of the ancient wisdoms and sciences were rewritten by every Christian Emperor — Augustus, Constantine I and II, Justinian, Charlemagne. All of them rewrote all of these truths that the ancient sects in the days of Yeshua ben Joseph — that lived near Jerusalem and in the cursed Valley of the Dead near the Dead Sea — had recorded these ancient myths for generations! Recycled ignorance is a little truth blended with a lot of superstition. And the first fifteen hundred years every emperor-proclaimed Christian made it their duty to rewrite and reestablish law, to reestablish the fear of reason, to drive home the submission of each individual's duty to submit to "God's will." And they had to live by that word; that was the law. And they were given the instrument of instant death if they did not. And little by little the lights were going out. All of you in this room underwent these times and lived through those times.

Did you know that in the sixth century an entity by the name of Proclus taught openly that the earth was round and that it made its orbit around the yellow sun? Did you know that so successful had the suppression of ancient truth and sciences been obliterated that by the days of confusion, times of confusion — called very appropriately your Dark Ages — that during the time of the Dark Ages all Christians thought the world was flat. And yet before, ancient sciences knew it was round and openly taught it.

Do you know why it changed? Because the four corners that the angels stand on the earth means it "must be flat." Know you what the four angels are? You don't. Four levels of consciousness, everything created on the fourth level. So well had they put out the lanterns that the world was plunged into darkness, an insidious darkness. Know what the darkness was? Stagnated evolution and ignorance under the guise of holy tyrants.

Today these old emperors are revered as saints. They're held in esteem as holy, holy people, pillars of the foundation of the church and all religion. But what these people did was a crime against the evolution of every single soul in its journey home. It detoured, collapsing reason and light, freedom, and equality and, above all, a God its life, and that which perceives it.

Now here are entities who rolled out the universes. Here are entities that have so much power they can love and have grace. They are creators. And the ancient wisdoms laid down in the Book of Life called Involution will be salvaged, and it is the only truth that will take you through the changes that the whole universe is in the throes of. So be it.

So what about real life? You're having problems living. It's because this is the most suffocating civilization there ever was. And my times of the Ram were glory days. You can only fantasize and perhaps snatch a fragment of a forgotten dream of what those days were like.

So successful were the last two thousand years in collapsing you into insecure people that you're very controllable. And you are very controllable by fear. It's been very arduous to teach you, knowing what to say to you and what not to say to you based on how you're going to react to it. How much fear do you still have within you? Can you take knowledge as the abstract objective and create it and make it subjective? Or do you take abstract knowledge and it threatens you, your sense of propriety and identity? Does it threaten your savings account, your stocks and bonds? Does it threaten your unhappy relationships?

What do I tell you? How do I gingerly, delicately, and with some candor, expose you little by little to truth, that you don't run away — because you're conditioned to do that — and beige out and become a dying ember? How do I tell you, supposedly in your society of modern conveniences, that you have nothing to fear, when you know full well you could starve tomorrow? Thus is the plight of one who leaves the land.

So how do I teach you knowledge abstractly? Did you know I addressed a window to your God of what was coming? A host of my runners has already materialized. Nature has spoken and is speaking. But how could I not show it to you? The few of you who remain in this room and the few who are not here are like the seeds that went through the fires of fear to own hope, a reality. And so many ran away. "The Ram is scaring everyone." How do I teach you without moving you from that place? How do I instruct you, to say, "You are the lights who are on that magnificent journey"?

There are some of you that have come here only waiting to see if the world is going to end in May. If it doesn't, you're going to go back to your way of life. That bespeaks an entity coming from 2,000 years of dense programming, to throw away all this truth because billions didn't die in a cataclysm. How about you? All it was worth was their hide; that was it.

Now I told you a lot of things this day. I said, "Sit and just listen." And I let it roll, roll. And not too many got frightened. Most were nodding in agreement. Well, then, why did you stop nodding when I said, "Change is the inevitable process of creation"? You nod when you know you're getting glorified but you stop when the earth starts to change.

I didn't come to be your baby sitter. I didn't come to be your spiritual guru. And I didn't come to be famous. I already am. I didn't come to make everyone like me. I came to teach them to do that for themselves. And I didn't come to walk on eggshells because I may offend you or scare you to death.

I came to slowly address you and build who you are, reminding you constantly never to forget who you are, to shine a reflection to you, that what see you in I is the potential of that which you are, to love you into life, to know that you are loved, that your voice is heard on the wind, that you have importance and value and credence to that which I am.

But to light the lantern again, to get you to a point to say, "Now that you're Gods who are at the end of page three, let us begin and turn to page four in the Book of Evolution and let us understand who and what your destiny is. You are mature enough spiritually; you have burned enough of the image away to handle the truth."

I have to tell you what the destiny of nature is. It is already programmed matter! I have to tell you what options are according to that. And time — listen to me — the unknown, is progressive creation! No one knows its time! It progresses in the spiral! In every downturn of the spiral consciousness is creating from subconscious mind, matter from antimatter, reality in the next move! Anyone can foretell the future of someone living in the groove. No one can foretell the future of one who is progressing into the unknown.

And the picture is "things are changing" — not tomorrow morning at 8:55 but they are changing. Your world is changing. The tyrants of old are making moves on these long, long centuries of programming. I lost so many telling them that. And in the vacuum, teachers and gurus sprang up with arms opened wide. Remember where tyrants come from? Where do they come from? Insecurity. Understand?

Now this ancient wisdom has everything to do with who you are today and who you are going to be in ten years. And knowledge is the lantern that lights the path in the darkness so that you can see the footprints that have been laid down so clearly by someone who loves you, to follow all the way through, no matter what is going on, that you're going to survive it all.

What does ancient wisdom, consciousness and energy, have to do with your love life, have to do with your money problems, have to do with your friendships, have to do with everything in your life, how you look? Because the "why" of all those things is the "how" of consciousness and energy. And they are your reality that you've created. You just didn't know how to go to the next step to resolve each of them, that they could become a wisdom instead of a mistake, that they become an experience, enriching, stretching you into virtue. In this day of struggling identities, knowing who you are, when everyone struggles to be more beige than the other, you'll be a light, an individual.

You're making changes in your life. The conditioning says you're not supposed to. The conditioning is to say, "That is selfish. You should not do that." But is not to love another the result of loving oneself? And is not a virtuous mind the result of an experienced being? Yes. And is life not the greatest teacher there is? Yes, because it is the probable unknown being realized every moment by you who are consuming it.

Now the "Days to Come" are still on and they're still happening. The ancient wisdom is coming back into proportion, the lights are coming on. Because it is the light that will take you through; not the ignorance and the fear and the superstition that holds you and says, "That's God's will that's happening there. And if you die, that's God's will. Don't question that." Fool! Who do you think God's will is? Who creates reality? You! And if you are homeless, that must be your karma! Bull! Causation is consciousness and energy and the friction of reality. That is purpose. It is creation!

Now you have only not to live in fear but to live according to the voice that is within you, this that is within you, that made you come here, that wanted you to come here. And all along the image is finding every reason why you shouldn't come. What did you listen to? This. Yes, because that which is listening loves that which I am because that which it is I am as well. That is what I am speaking to.

All you have to do is to listen to this knowledge. It will burn away and allow this truth to shine, this lantern to be lit. And no matter what is going on, you have an appointment with destiny, you radical few who in these times do not prepare because of fear but because you have to and you must complete the destiny of the soul, the Book of Life, all the way to page seven! And you have to live in this body to get there. Because you must fulfill the Book of Evolution in physical mass; that is its drama. You're not preparing to save your hide or because I told you to but because you should want to! Because it is the truth that bespeaks you inside.

That is what ancient wisdom and the ancient schools always taught: Never to forget and never get caught in the emotional drama that you forget who you are! Never mistake the character for self, never. And the same is happening now. Do not mistake change for the destruction of self. Do not forget who you are but to move through it; not with fear but with knowledge and truth and understanding.

Yeshua ben Joseph said a great truth that has been used in some quarters unfavorably — well, that is their lesson. The truth was, "If your arm defies you, cut it off. If your eye sees evil, pluck it out." Now what is behind that statement? What is behind the statement is, "Don't forget who you are. The kingdom of heaven is within you; the glory of God is within you. That which is God, you are, and if your body begins to defy you, cut it off." Meaning own it, get rid of it, burn away the image if it blocks this light.

Now many men castrated themselves, from the time of St. Augustine, holy men, for the name and the glory of Christ. And they castrated themselves that they would not have to address this "energy problem" they have. And they took the meaning of Yeshua ben Joseph as literal, that if they were haunted by the demons of their loins, they cut them off. But some of the most brilliant men came from that castration. They have come back, needless to say, this day as very passionate philosophers. This is a true story!

But Yeshua ben Joseph, Jesus the Christ, was saying a truth. If you know something to be, that is created for the purpose of your expression, interact with it but don't become it. And if something keeps pushing your buttons and you're doing it intentionally to yourself and you're in the habit of making yourself unhappy, get rid of it. If you're troubled by decadence, don't enterprise in it. If you are riddled with self-doubt, get rid of the one who tells you you should have self-doubt! Get rid of them! If you don't love what you are and think you're not beautiful enough, get rid of the things that intimidate you. Burning the image away, all things that hold it into beingness.

This ancient wisdom is more applicable in this density than it ever was before, ever. And the only temples that are left are the temple within and this gathering place, and a few others around your world who teach in secret places the same truth to initiates, pilgrims.

There's something very glorious in store for you. And it is not that you should sacrifice to have it. Change should not be a sacrifice; it should be a natural reaction to consciousness. Do you understand?

What was the beginning sentence that said, "Creation is..." what? Ah, you listened. Yes, it is a process. This should be a process, that you're evolving, that you're changing. Not that you have to; it just is. Do you understand?

Now everything that you have learned here this day will free you from everything in your life because you will perceive it as a reality you've created. So be it! And that's all you have to do, is to realize that you created it. And you did. And every block that stands in your way has been excuses not to know. And if you look at them and say, "I am no longer afraid, for I understand, I have knowledge," you can dissolve the blocks away to let the shine of that which you are spring forth. It will be like a river.

And those problems that haunt you, understand you're creating them and they're coming back to you because they're waiting for you to say, "Tell me what I taught you. You created me, now why? Tell me why." Ask them and then look and say, "Why did I create you?" And your God is going, "Yeah!" Yes, this is a very large, humbling experience. But you can find out because the moment you dare to answer the question then you no longer are the victim — do you understand? — and the reality of a victim. You are a God, a master, and it will tell you. And the moment you realize that, your consciousness will grow and expand and the lights are going on, and today's real world is going to change. Then the entity is born again, born again. You died in an image; you are born again in God within. So be it.

Now if this is seen like fresh water to you, it is. It is waters of life; you know, creation and its glory are being realized every moment. And God is awakening every moment to its whole potential, what it is. And you'll realize that your karma never existed and that your destiny was only one destiny and that was to be all you can be, which is in the Book of Life waiting to be experienced.

Most of you in this audience got this message this day. And already you are going through the frictions of the sentences of what you heard. You are reacting to them. That's wonderful; we have done wonderfully. But you will live through all of these times that are coming — the hailstones from afar, the rotating of the planet — you'll live through the comings and goings of land masses and all that goes on in change that is physical. Now I didn't say that is going to happen tomorrow but just that it is in the works. It's happened over and over and over again. And it always happens at the end of a great civilization. Did you know that?

So with knowledge and this little teaching on how you create your reality, the nature of reality, you became aware of the spiral of time — matter and antimatter, consciousness and subconsciousness — to how you create destiny and for what reason that you do. And that person that is very special to you in your life is really just a reflection of who you are now — and isn't that wonderful? — and vice versa; you to them.

And in this understanding that you have gained here this day, the more knowledge that you are aware of, the more you see that there really aren't any problems; there are only probabilities, and that the unknown really exists. And the unknown is what beckons you to discovery, to genius, to the potential of what you are. It's not a metaphysical superstition because in this unknown does not lie the polarities of good and bad and negative and positive or higher and lower; that's dogma. It is. It is not a dark force and a light force. There is only light. Darkness is simply ignorance. That's all.

There are grand things to be experienced out there that are waiting for you. But this knowledge that you've heard is going to take time — the rolling of consciousness into subconsciousness, the rolling of matter into antimatter — to create reality because everything you've heard you must experience. It must be the nature of your reality this day forward.

So on the spiral, on the time flow, you are now booked up five years in advance, regardless of what or anything that goes on. The power of this being is that it has willed itself to learn, to experience. It has a purpose to live for five years. The lights are back on and the flame is glowing.

So how does one will oneself into the future? By coming back to the simple truth of what you are and what your purpose is. How can anyone give up on life and find no reason to live when the adventure of the unknown beckons and the God within is crying out to do it? One who gives up on life is collapsed by the social standards around them that they are a participant within.

How can you not want to live? Do you not know that the beings that are beyond the sun that live for tens of thousands of years as one singular person do so because they willed themselves to?

Do you have life insurance policies? Are you betting you're going to die? Are your beneficiaries checking up on you? Don't you understand that's a reality created by consciousness?

These beings have understood how consciousness and energy create the nature of reality and how progressive self is all important to the whole. It's their duty to awake the sleeping God. They've willed themselves to be ten thousand years old. And what did I say? If that isn't truth, then everything that I've said is a fantasy.

In the nature of reality, if you can see how you've created, then how can you stretch that consciousness with knowledge to make an appointment with destiny ten years away? Can you do it? You did it in this audience just by sitting and listening and being, because I declared it will take you five years to experience it. So be it.

Now will; will your reality. Will it to be flexible, to unleash consciousness. Will change to be. Walk away from yesterday, for the past lies in the book that is covered in the first three pages. It's open to page four. You don't have to go back and review. That is the past; leave it alone. And you start now with taking hold of this destiny and what you think is.

An abstract thought? Well, what is abstract thought, people, especially in these turbulent times when no one has a rational answer for anything? Abstract thought is the ability to start on the spiral with your back to the past — meaning the past is now the present. It no longer exists in time; it is now. And consciously invoking — with the desire to invoke the subconscious mind — which means you're calling forth the Is to come forth into realization. And the moment you call it forth, it is an unknown that has no emotional attachment because emotional attachment is the result of the interaction created in your reality. It is unemotional. Abstract thoughts are the probability that exist in the one vast nothing materially. And you start the movement in mind.

And as you project out the light begins to stretch over the darkness or the thought. And it is coming up into consciousness, and the entity begins to make a descent in that splendor of a moment. And there is a flash of antimatter and there is a flash of subconscious mind that responds. And the magnetism, the magnetism, is the journey back up to the next blurp, that is the manifested reality coming from subconscious mind that creates the nature of reality. And in the next blurp you experience it in your life, have an emotional reaction and it is recorded as wisdom, and you are on the road to genius. And that's how you do it! And that is all you have to do.

The abstract is opening up and pulling from nothing something. Get it? It has no dogma, no laws attached, no fine print. It just comes. It is being made known; it's turning into light. That is thinking in the abstract; that is stretching in the abstract. It is not sitting there wearing your emotions on your sleeve crying out, "Help me!" And when the thought comes you don't listen because it doesn't say, "Woe is you!" You just embrace it, and it comes.

And this mind begins to open. It is activated. The hormone flow is

The Destruction of Ancient Wisdom and Its Resurrection — Afternoon Session

flowing into the brain, the mind is beginning to ache and to burn; the body is heating up in fire. There is something happening in manifested energy — what the magnetism that comes out of subconscious mind into reality is — that it is taking form in time and the magnetism says it belongs to your life. You created it.

It's not hard to do that. All you have to do is want to. Every moment henceforth when you turn to the unknown, you pull from the unknown what it will give you in the next moment and you manifest it.

Now why am I telling you that? Because that is the knowledge of how things work in this life and there's nothing out there to be afraid of: There are no demons; there is no devil; there is no black hole; there is no white hole; there is nothing that is going to suck you out of gravity and hurl you through space! No. There are only the probabilities of all human potential. That's what it is.

And in the days that are coming, remember what I just told you here because that is the clue of how to keep living, to pull out, willing that there is purpose every moment you embrace it. And every moment you embrace it, the life is expansive and more creative and more dynamic. And who would want to die on a life like that? No, because the ultimate that you are to become is God-man/God-woman realized. Realized! There have been no women Christs in your civilization. In these times there is coming a host that will become God-woman realized, the density of a great mastery, and that is called Christ.

You have learned?

Listen. This may be unexplainable to you when it occurs, so I wish to tell you. Because of the dynamics of what you're learning, you know this organism here (the brain)? It's going to open up. It had to open up to hear what you heard this day. Now there is whole physical science about how the brain becomes a lot of highways for ingenious thought. In every small tissue it's waiting to be impregnated. The brain is like a great womb waiting to be seeded with the dynamics of unknown possibilities. We latched onto it. Allow that thought coming from the unknown to make its way all the way through the brain. And it does do that; it breaks ground and circuits.

Do you remember when I said to you there were no seven levels, only the seventh, until you began? And you had to create these levels as you lowered in evolution? The brain is waiting to be impregnated by thoughts that will create levels in the brain to facilitate thought. They're like highways. And every great unknown thought you have penetrates the brain mass and imprints on it. It makes an electrical highway that leaves its imprints, that a similar thought can now be picked up on this highway into new territory. How else do you think things become familiar to you? How could you read another person's thought unless you already had this pattern already sitting there?

Well, what we want to do is to take a very large brain and make it look like a road map. You know a road map? And every moment that you consciously embrace — which is every day, in particular now — you realize that you're just creating. You can't help it; it just is there! But every moment you stretch and will that mind to consume more of the subconscious mind, you're causing highways to occur up here.

Well, now hold on. What begins to happen is there is a place where they all crisscross from the frontal lobes of the brain. You know, it's sitting in half — you know that — only because there is this little flower sitting between them. It's called the pituitary. Well, it's not where they cross; it's that gland that opens up and secretes the hormone that activates another part of the brain so these unknown thoughts can enter. That pituitary in genetic mass has been closed very tightly for a very long time. And when it starts to open genetically it hurts. So your head is going to hurt, throb between your eyes. So bless it. Take two aspirin. It will be wonderful!

But that's not what I'm speaking about. All of these inroads cross through a nerve center and they cross the part of the brain that sits right back here. And there is a little mass in there that is a section all by itself where all of these highways crisscross. Now remember when I said to you that the earth was like a ball of twine of electrical current? That every place that crossed was a blurp of matter and, when you look at it, you think it's all solid? Well, it really isn't.

Now so as above, so below. In this, you have this little point where everyone of these highways begin to cross. And in this area is a highly charged section of the brain that has been dormant genetically in this species of this civilization. And this area is the area that, when all of the crossings of these highways in the brain occur, allows you to dissolve the dimensions.

And it is the part that is so sensitive it picks up the frequency of higher vibrations; therefore the veil comes off. And you can see what others cannot see. As I am sitting here, you can see what I really look like. And by the time you've earned the right to do that, you'll appreciate me and not worship me. You'll earn the right to be able to watch the "ghost walk," the people walking to and fro, caught up in their identities; you'll be able to observe them. You'll be able to observe the lights in the heaven, the interdimensional people who live right along with you. You'll be able to look at a person and know exactly what they're thinking because when the veil comes down you have dominion over all areas. And that potential in mass sits right here.

Those people were called the great visionaries, the great seers, oracles. And they could see what you could not see. They're the ones who first spoke of fairies and small illuminated beings and the entities that lived close to the plant world. They were very small people. You think that the wee people are a myth? No, they exist, but only the visionaries ever saw them.

Now there is a word that was given to a very few people over your time and it was called the Illuminated Ones. And then it got to be called the Great White Brotherhood, which is a sort of a bigotry in name because there is also the Great Black Brotherhood and there's the Great Green Brotherhood and there's a Great Brown Brotherhood and there's the Great Red Brotherhood; you understand? And then there are the Sisterhoods, all different colors! Well, remember, everything is a reality!

So the reason that I'm educating you a little bit about this, and perhaps dragging this out a bit, is because this is a process that begins on page four and really hooks in on page five in the book. But during these next five years you're going to have some dreams and you're going to see lights off of the side of your face and you're going to turn and look at them. The cone in the eye cannot decipher them, but they're there and they dance. And no matter how you endeavor to look on them directly, they are not relative to your limited eye; they are relative to this. Do you understand?

And you will be walking along — and hopefully not in a city street — and you'll hear a conversation of two women and they'll be walking on seemingly a light, yet it is solidity, just above you. And they're walking through a forest and they're carrying on the most delightful conversation in laughter. God, they are beautiful. And their laughter is like a golden melody laced upon the wind of time. And you'll look and you'll see them and you're going to be awestruck. And they'll walk on. And as they walk on, their path rolls up behind them. They didn't even acknowledge you but you got to see them in their world. And they live in a world that is so far from this place, yet is the same in thought.

You're going to have fireballs come overhead and they'll blaze through the sky. And you're going to say, "Did you see that?"

"Huh?" And they didn't! And they don't even believe you! And you will encounter mystical things and behold the mystic! Now that is because of the crossing that is an inevitable side effect in evolving. Do you understand?

Now there is so much magic, like the day I became the wind and in a moment I was out of my body — way above looking down; seeing the speck; feeling detached. But I had never ridden in an aeroship and yet there I was. And fear overtook me and the next moment, back I was! What allowed that to happen in that moment? It happened so quickly. I didn't sit and contemplate that; I never knew it existed. It was an unknown. So how did an unknown entice the Ram to get out of his body? In just one pure moment, that nothing else existed except that moment, I became in that moment antigravity and subconscious mind; in one moment.

You're going to find yourself walking along and it will seem that you're not touching the ground. And you're going to have a dream about flowing out of the window. You'll hear this scream. It is the death of the image and the freedom of the spirit. And in that moment you're at the other side of the moon. In a moment! It's there, now; it is! And you'll be like the wind. That is what waits out here, in this place that no one wanted you to go because of the tyrants of insecure people who could not evolve. They have stagnated the glory and the majesty of what an electrifying being you are. And all that awaits you.

Listen to me. In the last part of the schools it was such a sentence that took on such a life that for that entire year the experience was lived, and lived over until the moment came they could levitate from this space to that space, because it was breaking down images and freeing up consciousness. You see, it is only your reality that says you can't do it. It is the unknown that says all probabilities exist.

It's not that you sit and eat the right food, drink the right water. It's not that you wear crystals. Because I will tell you, you can get a bigger charge in sticking your finger in one of those plugs than you can wearing a crystal! Shock of your life! Nothing; you don't have to do any of that. That is dogma. All you have to do is know, be in knowledge and let this great consciousness work. And you won't have to sit down and say, "I'm going to leave my body." It just happens in a moment. That is what this inside wants to experience in this. Understand?

Now that is my P.S. — postscript of the Ram — because it's not something you have to run around and say, "Why is this happening to me?" Never ask why and excuse yourself from the delirium of light or genius. And you don't have to want to be that so you'll be somebody. You already are! Some *body*, indeed!

And don't be a fanatic about this business — there are more fanatics that live in this little town. I love everyone of them but they're still — I would not want to sit down and dine with them and don't! Well, why did I say that? Only because they've taken snatches of the ancient wisdom — like the man who needed the strokes — and made them into something without taking the whole sentence. At least listen to the whole sentence. In the ancient schools that is why one great teaching lasted a year! That you didn't run off — what is it — half-cocked? And if you're half-cocked, it ain't happening.

You had to take the whole sentence and it's like a reel of film. You can see the beginning of the first frame of this film and you can see the last frame, but it takes a year for you to see it; that's how the teachings were. So that there was no one who just took and snatched a glimmer; they lived completely each frame of that film of that sentence.

Now that's what engaged their knowledge and that's what prohibited superstition. And the intent was to continue to learn that "I can create out here all that I need to experience."

So here in one day you've gone through a myriad of years. No wonder you go off half-cocked because you didn't listen to the first word and hear the last word, as well, and everything in between. And you hold onto that and it becomes your reality and it's incomplete! Now in this little town there is a lot of half-cocks. And it is not that this is where fanatics come. No, that is only relative to one's perception of it. But it is entities who exalt themselves on a fragment of the truth rather than hearing the whole truth; do you understand?

Now where was this leading? Oh, yes. There's a lot of talk but nothing's happening and that is because the talk of the incomplete truth goes on and there's no acting upon it. So there are no inroads happening up here, and there is no illumination going; there is only repeating happening.

Now in this film that I told you about — it is a wonderful demonstration, for I was privileged to see celluloid. And people who live in the groove are like the strip of celluloid. And when you unroll it, you can see their beginning and their end. But when you put it through a machine, it rolls like matter, constant, a whole lifetime. But the end is very clear.

What you're going to learn, that is going to open all of this up and bring this into wonderful alignment, is those spaces in between the frames, you know, when they send you back negatives and there's no picture on it and you go, "It didn't take!" and you throw them away! Subconscious mind, the great nothing materially but all things potentially, went into the garbage! Now this, in-between-the-frames, is the unknown. It is questing for that vision that opens all of this up.

Now why did the interactions of mind that span the entire universe cease? When those who left, who turned their faces to the sky — that said, "Watch for me, I'll be back" — and the corruption and the disassembling of the ancient science was now occurring, the deterioration of purpose also created entities who stopped growing here who could break down distance and space just by consciousness that allowed this interaction. There was no one living here anymore that wanted to have an interaction. Everyone was busy killing everyone.

As you begin to progress in this, you're going to call back that friendship. And those great stones that are saying, "Watch for me. I'm coming back," they do come back when this opens up and the communications are open and you have a friendship and a camaraderie with Gods from all sorts of places and all sorts of shapes. And that is a part of these truths that you learned this day. And they have an appointment with you in the next five years because that is also destiny. So be it.

To the lanterns.

How do you know that all of this is truth? How could this be true? You can see it in your life and you feel it in here, don't you know? That what can be perceived as a possibility can and is a reality. So everything that you just heard this day is your reality, now.

That is all! Yes, indeed!

THE SEVENTH SEAL AND THE COMPLETED GARMENT OF LIGHT

MORNING SESSION

I am very honored! My army never applauded me; they just all got drunk!

I am very honored that the lot of you have made your way, time, egos-altered and otherwise, to come here. It does my being great wonders to see you all gathered. I love each of you who have come to learn knowledge, for there is nothing else you are going to get here. And yet with that it makes everything else possible.

From the Lord God of my Being,
Unto the Glory within,
Unto that which be I,
Glorify me this day.
Bring down the walls
And allow the power
And truth
To be lived,
Unto this day
And to the glory of God
I am.
So be it.

The Ancient Schools of Wisdom

Yes. In the day that was called yesterday, that is now understood to be the past in your time as you know it, an audience was held here that addressed the ancient wisdoms and their demise. And the day prior to that, that is now history in the now, a teaching was addressed that was called "The Nature of Reality."

In those days, in the nature of reality in the ancient schools, it would have taken one year to have learned. And you would have lived at the ancient school in order to have learned it. It wasn't that you come, learn a little bit, go out and have food stuffs and wine and go shopping.

It was a school of the initiates, an intense school, that was created for the Gods who comprise the two principles of all life, consciousness and energy, that were demonstrated in the form of man and woman in this journey through dense mass and awakening matter, for them to remember the purpose for their journey.

Now every teaching lasted a year. And the year was different than in your time and counting. You're operating from a different calendar than existed then, but the fact is that it took a whole year. In one day a profound collection of hieroglyphics or words was given to the students and in a very special place — the form of the fiery form — and that whole day they would expand and stretch their consciousness to consume that sentence. By the end of the day they could manifest it out of their hands.

Well, that teaching, that was the first day of these collections of ancient wisdoms in yesteryear, lasted a year. And those wonderful pilgrims that came here, students, got it in one day. Well, that's all right. Now also understand it still will take a year to unfold in the time flow the revelation and the manifestation of each complete sentence that was taught.

Because this is not a school of philosophy and spiritual teachings — that is such an empty phrase — but it is a school where the words represent the diligence of an unfolding God to consume the glory of what life is and its experiences and to make them happen. So the words are imperative to stretch consciousness and for each God to make that word a manifested experience, that each word could be recorded in their book, their soul, of life. So the students, the pilgrims of that day, would live a year of every sentence every day and all they had to do was sit and listen.

The Seventh Seal and the Garment of Light — Morning Session

Now the pickle in this barrel was they came back the next day, and the next day was called "The Ancient Wisdoms and their Demise." Well, altogether those two days would have lasted five years to understand in the ancient schools. So the pilgrims that came here the first day have a sentence of the first day every day and a sentence three different times of the second day. So it is needless to say that the learnings that they're going to have are going to be quite intense. I want them to be because you can't have an ancient school and make it fluffy and on your terms.

So now here you are, with a growing audience coming this day, "The Great Seventh Seal And Adorning The Arraignment Of Light, The Garment Of The Completed Soul." So now these days have equaled seven years of teaching of old.

And by this day the student would have, in the past, progressed to the level that in the seventh year the initiate was ready for extraordinary manifestation. And whereas it challenges you to sit and be quiet, because silence is an alienation to you — to be alone to some of you is very frightening — the initiate by the seventh year had learned so profoundly to be an adept in the silence that it could pull from subconscious mind the absolute and work it every day.

Yeshua ben Joseph was an initiate of the ancient schools and one of the last that existed.

So here you are, not having lived the previous years and working up to this day. The ten years that some of you have been involved in this teaching has been to address the needs and problems and difficulties, so that to say you are God becomes a meaningful thing to you. It has taken this long to begin to wake you up and to show you that change isn't the end of the world; it is the beginning of awakening.

So here we have an audience that has not lived through seven years of the ancient schools. To be an initiate that could sit in an audience in absolute silence and open that mind and stretch and pull superconsciousness through, you couldn't do it. But in seven years you will. So be it.

So this day will have to be words and the words are very powerful. They are stretching your reality. The nature of your reality is getting very fat, very large and very luminous. Your knowledge is growing. And wherever your knowledge grows, your reality must equal.

So you're going to sit and listen this day; that's all you're going to do. You're going to listen and you're going to stretch and you're going to have visions plop before your eyes. You're going to be reminded of things that are going on in your life. You're going to have buttons pushed in your soul. Some will get angry, some will weep, some will be mystified, and some will stay, fighting to keep their attention because their image is wanting to turn them off.

For whatever you learn this day, what you hear is the unfoldment of the next seven years. You have an appointment with destiny as a result of being here this day. And that no matter what happens in the days to come that are already here, you're going to live through at least seven years. Because in the time-space-matrix spiral of matter/antimatter, consciousness and subconscious mind, you have an appointment in seven years to have fulfilled this learning this day. So be it.

And because this learning pulls you off of the wheel and puts you into that spiral of time — the manifestation of consciousness, ever-increasing consciousness, increasing reality — you're not going to have an accident and you're not going to die of disease, because you are willing yourself to be what you hear this day. So be it.

Before we begin this, I want to say something about you. I want this message to go to you as an individual because though there are many people in this room — and some are individuals and some are struggling to be individuals — this message is for you personally. Just like the fall of spirit and this magnificent journey into the unknown pulling out of the Is or subconscious mind to make conscious reality, this is a long and arduous and very painful journey.

I would like to remind you that the splendor that you are — powerful consciousness, powerful energy that once were like lights that lit up levels of vibrations — is seven of those levels lowered, lowered, and lowered in your soul according to your book called Involution. You created the seven levels that have brought you to this density of mass. You have awakened dead matter with your intelligence.

I want you to know something. It has been a painful, arduous and, at times to some, a regrettable journey. Because the magnificent Gods that you are, that truly unwielding energy can be wielded and concentrated in areas to unfold the universe. Yes, you can do that. You have made a journey into a dimension that involves time, living through a body that must live according to that time, with a mind so powerful that it is captivated in the skull and its body cannot keep up with the thoughts that it thinks.

Now what kind of an intelligence are you that can sit under a weeping willow and have prose and poetry come to you that is so majestic and so riveting that it bespeaks who you are, forgotten Gods, or doing your daily chores, living a life of mediocrity and yet having a soul that is more profound than the stars in the heavens? And there is no one who has made a journey quite like the journey you're all on.

I know what you are and what you're made out of; I've been you. I am standing at the other end of this tunnel with the light beckoning you through it, through all of the darkness and the terror and the screams and disease and pestilence and the social consciousness and the anger and bitterness and the betrayals and hypocrisies, and lies, hardships. And you have had hardships. I want you to know I know you have.

Well, what is it that drives you on? What is it that can talk about a sunset in such splendor it's as if you'd never seen it before and had seen it for the first time? And what is it that can weep at the sounds of a night bird or feel a wind, not chilling but caressing? That's what I know you are, that unseen essence that keeps you going on that brought you to the audience to see this incredulous thing occur. But as incredulous as I am, it is what you all are.

It has been very painful, this journey to go home. And then wondering if it's all a fantasy. Is it all some cruel truth or myth perpetrated upon you? No, the cruel truth is to say it doesn't exist. The truth is it does.

I never came here to instigate followers and I don't want you to be that. There are others that are waiting for that. I didn't come here to stroke you or tell you incredulous truths about who you were in past lives or to give you amulets and rocks and crystals and trinkets to pacify you so that you think you've got something. I came here with a message that wasn't even shocking but little by little to awaken something that is what I am, to get you out of the murk and mire and let you see what you are, to see something rather splendid within you, something whose possibilities are unconditional love and grace and truism. The potential for a brilliant light lies in each one of you, that you didn't collapse into a consciousness that was just the grave and the worm.

Listen you. I came back here to light the lanterns again, that imageless God that you are, that unidentifiable character, polishing it and building your confidence in yourself, helping you take each step into the unknown to show you, "Create your reality different, you've made it here. Look at what it's taught you and your kingdom will broaden." You've been through a lot of pain, a stifled being who has a desire to go to the other side of the sun but is limited by time, distance, space, mass.

I came to tell you the truth and I've addressed everything you've created in this life, much to many's dismay, but I came here. And most of you stood by this truth, in a whirling vortex of confusion and an angry nation, angry families. And you stood by your truth, unwielding, unyielding, to come here this day. You went through your fires and your dark night of the soul. Now how do you think that a broadsword is tempered? How do you think the metal is tempered and strengthened?

You're worthy to be in this audience, even if it will last seven years, because it has said a lot for you to be here and I love you for that. Those lights in the lanterns — the old lanterns, not like these — were lit with oil. And over time I have seen them break and the oil spill upon the barren earth and the light extinguished. There are many who live without lights within them; they are the living dead because they have yielded completely to the character they created, and the forgotten God is a dying ember. And here the lights have been lit again and they waver in the wind, but there is a fire, a flame, a torch burning.

If this isn't truth then all you have to look forward to is the grave and the worm. But the light inside says, "Tis so, I know it;" that's why you're here.

Well, I am grateful for you. I have been a very strong teacher, yes. And, yes, harsh. What do you expect out of an image that was a barbarian? And what do you expect out of a conqueror who says, "Why are you sitting here weeping over this? Take the sword out and cut it down!" Yes. And why do I say to you, "Change. It's not going to hurt you! And if it does, you need it!"

And, no, I am not a "mamby-pamby." I do not speak as a woman and I do not whisper as a man. I am the Ram! And I don't fit anyone's boxes! Because I am here on my father's business, which happens to be your business. But throughout it all what remains, and the representatives of that remaining, are in this audience.

There are many out there who couldn't come here but they're going to hear this recorded message and your response and they're going to feel your energy. And wherever they hear this, they too have entered the ancient schools so the lanterns are going on everywhere.

And the only way that you change reality is to gain the knowledge that engages it. And that is what this audience and these days and all of these years have been about. I have saved the best for last!

These learnings are the prelude to the next ten years. But you had to have earned the right for the next ten years, and that is being humbled enough to say, "What I want is knowledge." Know you what the wise man desires? Know you what the wise woman desires? Knowledge.

So wonderful God-men, God-women, recipient of all my runners, with your love and perseverance you're on your way home. And though seemingly the future holds pain for a lot of people, it will not hold it for you because knowledge is the healer of darkness and misunderstanding. So be it.

Now just listen, that's all you have to do, just listen. For the way that you create reality is to experience an unknown. I am going to tell you a lot of unknown things this day. So you're having an opportunity to engage an unknown potential, that the moment you understand it, the moment you hear it, it begins the process on the spiral of going down and being manifested from subconscious mind. The matter, or the reality of it, is manifested from antimatter. The magnetism pulls it up to be created in reality. And when it happens, you experience it and your reality grows. So is the way of a genius.

Now in the ancient schools there was no ritual. There was "ohming" and a hum and there was quiet. For nothing that you can do is greater than to take knowledge and to be with it. It is the greatest illuminator there is!

What you hear this day you will have plenty of opportunity to be with it. And you'll know every day, as it starts to work in your reality. The soul is not God. The soul is the book in which all of your experiences are recorded upon. God is the Spirit that you are, Spirit, the super intelligence of consciousness and energy that brings dead matter alive, and that wherever you put your focus, reality begins to come alive.

There are a lot of you in this audience that did not hear how you create the nature of your reality. That's a very important teaching because without it you cannot understand what it is you're going to hear this day. And you can't understand about ancient teachings without the nature of reality that furthers you to understand about the seventh seal. So I'm going to give you a short, short, refresher course. This is what you call "cash and carry?" Quick.

Think about this: The subconscious mind is not the accumulated experiences that you've been taught. The subconscious mind is the one vast nothing materially — now listen — but all things potentially. The subconscious mind is called the Is. It is the void in space. It is the giver of all life. But it is one vast nothing materially, yet it is the all-in-all of realized material potentials. So potentials, probabilities, adventure, experience, unknown realities await in the one vast nothing called the Is, which has been referred to as God, and yet God comes from the Is.

Now consciousness is conscious Is. Consciousness is awakened intelligence; the Is is sleeping potential. Are you with me? Splendid. Now when the Is moved — and this is a parable of what occurred — it moved, contemplated itself, and in one moment light filled the void. And light is made up of light particum. A singular, individual light source comprises the whole of light.

Now that light — think about this — is a light in which the Is, or the subconscious mind, is flowing into and that little dot of light particum is awakened consciousness and that Is keeps flowing to that little light particum. And it's awakened. It's stirring. It is aware. It is an aware intelligence.

Now the moment it awakened and became light, it created a soul. A soul is an energy. It's not really a book, but a book is the grandest way to ascribe what it is. And the soul had the specific ability to record every stir, and the moment consciousness stirred, it recorded it. The moment it was recorded, energy was born, and energy is the active ingredient. It is the handmaiden of consciousness that constitutes the nature of reality. Now we have a living being that is called "God." Every one of you in this audience is that light particum. Every one of you are comprised with the only two principles that existed in an amoral, objective, universal Is. Consciousness and energy are the light particum, the Spirit, the Gods, plural, that you are.

The reason for being? That it became the first page in your book that was entitled Involution. On page one in this book, what this consciousness and energy would do would be to create the destiny to make known the unknown, to consciously consume the subconscious mind, to create all life, reality. That is a superlative destiny.

The glory of creation in that splendid moment, that light, that particum, that energy, that which you are — listen to this so you remember this when you think your destiny is to heal the world — the glory was not in your creation; it was in the consumption of creation; to consume that Is, that subconscious mind, to make it real, to create reality from. It is not creation. And remember this: Creation is not an act; it is the process. It is like breathing. It is the life process of every God to create. You're not to sit there and float around as a wee, little light on this great darkness and just mind your own business. You are destined to consume and make life. You are destined to consciously make what is unconscious conscious.

And whatever you perceive in consciousness, your energy creates and when your energy creates it, it becomes reality; whatever you think becomes your reality. And your energy is there to make it manifest. Consciousness and energy, words and music. Consciousness and energy, the working principle of that which is termed Gods.

Now how did you get here when you were there? How did you get so dull when you used to be so brilliant? In the Book of Life, Involution, there was a conscious awareness to begin to delve into the subconscious mind and all of its layers of reality. And the seventh level was where it all began, and that which is termed the seventh page was that they would begin to manifest, through their consciousness, this light. They began to lower, to go to the next level. If you take thought and it contemplates itself, light is born. If you take light and lower it, it begins to get dimmer and its reality reflects a whole different reality. And these entities went to page six in their book and created the sixth dimension, the sixth level and all that was involved in creating that level. They explored in it consciousness and made it real through their energy. And when they owned that at the bottom of page six, they turned the page and went to page five and created that. Now remember, none of these levels existed. They were the yet-to-be-explored-and-made reality of the unknown mind. In other words, this was a journey of God awakening itself, to explore all that it is. And they did that all the way to page four.

And page four in involution is where the term epigenetics came from; that is how they awakened dead matter. And dead matter is the coagulated thought on level one, where you're at. And on page four they created the idealism that would become the chromosome genetic imprint in a single cell. That cell knows how to divide itself according to its chromosomes in its tree of genetics. There's a pattern; it has to complete that pattern. Every cell carries the pattern of the whole. A scraping of a cell of your body can be cloned to reproduce another body! Where did you think the intelligence came from that imprinted that tree?

The Tree of Life, that's what the chromosome tree is all about. Where did it come from? It came from the spirits, the fallen Gods, on the fourth level that created the pattern and the destinies of life.

And this glorious place called terra was once an exploding nova and before that it was light that was bursting — the Big Bang, "X-particum" — in the universe. It was existing in thought and was lowered, and then became the particums through rotation. But all the earth is is concentrated energy lines, coagulated thought. And everything on this earth was patterned intelligence set about in the time flow for evolution. Epigenetics is the spiritual design that would become dead matter awakened genetically. Are you with me? This is a very fast description for all of this.

Now on the fourth level, with everything set, these Gods began to lower to the third, then to the astral level, that which is a quickening vibration. It's the next vibration from this level. And there they moved across the deep like a wind. And, behold, the Gods took up the bodies of the children of the earth. And so you did.

Now the moment you became coagulated flesh in the first physical body you had, your book was turned over and the title of this book was called Evolution. You're on page one, first seal, copulation, survival. And, yes, you didn't come here in flowing garments. You looked like an ape, you smelled like an ape, and you walked like an ape. Darwin is correct. And the brain, only so large, was all that was needed for a first level entity. And yet, imagine for a moment, we are talking about something that was the first light is now this? But that is in reflection.

And guess what? This was beautiful to its creators. It didn't say, "This is ugly," and it didn't know it was supposed to smell like roses! It was just life; you understand? Life. And it began to create the reality by consciously embracing a concept, interacting with that concept, having an emotional experience with it; and, behold, a tree existed now and it was written down in their book.

And they learned all of these things that they would pass on instinctively through the chromosomes to the generations that would follow. And they would die, lay down that body and pick up another one ten thousand years later, because the brain has evolved and they're large enough to get into that brain and have another experience. Do you understand? Every page in the book was to evolve upon. And so they started moving right along.

And great, great civilizations started that way and went all the way to the seventh page, and they're gone now. And that has happened many times on this earth. It has happened many times in other parts of this your galaxy, that is a very far remote galaxy in comparison to other intelligence. And they evolved and went back home. They owned all of the density of matter, made it life, reversed the process, went all the way up through these seals and became illuminated Christ and returned to the thought as light. And the void is being lit up by them.

Now here you sit, modern man and woman. You smell excellent. Any hair that's not supposed to be there you remove or you culture. You walk upright. You wear fine silks, broadcloths, cloths of gold and silver, fine hair from the sheep. And just looking at you with all this brain mass up here, it would be assumed that you could do all of these things, that you're going to learn that you can do already, yet you're not.

And nature continued to evolve — it's way ahead of you. And this brain mass is very large but it is only a little bit used. And this body — to continue to be a character, to learn something so you could record it in your book, you now become this body. Grave error.

The ancient schools of wisdom were created for the Gods, for them to come back and to relearn what it is they came here to do and to tell you, "You're not your body. You're not needing to wear those windows. You're not really who you look like. It's not important how big you are, how virile you are. It doesn't matter who you're married to! The problems are not you!" And they would bring them in, and they would go to school and they would remember! "Ah, of course, how could I forget? Silly me!" But the moment that the ancient wisdom and all of the scales could come off of realization and go back to saying, "This is your destiny," then all of those illusions were absolved and the entity was able to go on and change and evolve.

Evolution doesn't mean being still; it means movement, does it not? And evolution also is time, is it not? And consciousness funded is evolving consciousness, meaning experienced, enriching.

So you got a little problem seven and a half million years ago when someone got very insecure because they couldn't get beyond the third seal, and they got very insecure and needed to be stroked.

I want you to listen very carefully. People who left this audience — because they needed that "personal contact," they needed to be recognized, they needed to feel like they were special, someone important — they left because they weren't getting it. Seven and a half million years ago there was a man who did not go to school all those moments that the entity should and didn't go there to get out of this, and he got stuck in this energy of the third seal, which is power. And power controls pain, and pain is the result of copulating Gods. So he got to feeling a little insecure, couldn't go to the next seal, couldn't discover love. Love doesn't exist here, entities, and neither does divinity! Man and woman consume life to create divinity; they're not born with it.

And what do insecure people do? Insecure people need to be loved; they need to be stroked. They are naturally possessive, jealous tyrants. And they start out innocently wanting attention. Why? Because there's nothing in here that they're allowing to give them that attention. They haven't evolved there. And so the entity made a proclamation to God. This voice that was talking to him inside was saying, "Turn the page! Go to school! You're sick, go to school! You have to listen to me! This is an experience. You must see it. You must own it. We must move from this place." And he says, "God is speaking to me," but he's not moving. So what does he do? He makes a proclamation that women will no longer be communicated to by God and that man would become the only representation of God! And the women, of course, having nothing in their book to say otherwise, agreed. It was the next adventure.

So the fall of women came. And they're locked in these areas here and man is locked in these areas here. And every lifetime civilization is being built on that cultural, civilized, exchange that women are subentities and servants and bitches and hetaera to men. And they can only attain God through being married or through a man or through a priest. I mean, God is a man, is he not? And his son was a man, and the holy ghost is a man, and the disciples were men. Who created that God? Well, you create God in your own image.

So seven and a half million years ago you started getting stuck.

Women didn't really realize they were women; they were simply Gods expressing. And men really didn't have to hold all of their energy in their penises; they were simply Gods expressing. They were innocent and yet on a journey, the most awesome journey ever. And someone created a reality that became truth, and everyone abided by it.

And now you have a stagnated civilization and you have sexual identity problems. Women are trying to be women even though they have this and this. Men are trying to be men even though they have this. They don't understand what it is they're lacking. What they are lacking is to see what they have owned there and move on.

So we have an identity crisis in this room. And the identity crisis is that every lifetime you lived, you have picked the genetic tree to return to, every situation you designed so that you could engage an unknown so that you could pull up from the subconscious mind an opportunity to experience, in the physical, a new reality, a new understanding, an illumination, a genius. That was your natural course. And when this life was finished, if you chose to lay that body down and wait ten thousand years and return and pick one up again, you would go forward and continue to embrace in mass, that you're turning those pages in your soul of evolution.

But all of a sudden, when women were women and men were men and God was a man and women were subject to the male desire, we stopped having that occur and identity became the issue, and you created a rut.

You are to create as a spiral. That is what the time-space matrix looks like, is a spiral. Matter/antimatter, consciousness/subconsciousness: time. That's how you create. But here, in thirty-five thousand years solidified, you're stuck in this groove and you've become the image. You've become that body: how you look, what color your eyes are, what color your hair is, how large your penis is, how big your breast is, how skinny you are, how fat you are, how you smell, how you are accepted in the community. You have become the density of mass and your consciousness has stopped growing; it is only relative to how you feel.

Did you ever ask your soul to go back in and review those pages? Well, you're reviewing them all the time in the groove. Have you ever asked your Spirit, your God within, how it feels? Well, you've got a bellyache, you got gas — but what about your Spirit? How does it feel? It just doesn't exist as "I identify only through my senses."

So here we have all of consciousness creating a reality that is pure physical. And you're stuck on page three in the Book of Evolution. And your God inside is saying, "Own this. You are greater than this. We have done this before. We have had this relationship before. You have labored at this before. You are dying. Wake up!"

And your image, your altered ego, says, "This is the thing to do. This is how you look. This is how you talk. This is how I'm supposed to feel. I'm 'in!' You're not supposed to think outrageous thoughts like that! How do you discuss them over lunch?"

So these bodies — that were only a vehicle for God to awaken through to know itself, for the light to consume the subconscious mind and pull from it that which makes reality — stopped growing and became physical, physical! Think about it! Think about it! The time it takes for you to unroll a universe, it takes to gargle. The same energy that it takes to create genius, you're thinking about what perfume you're going to wear. Consciousness and energy creates reality. And if your consciousness has created an image that becomes your reality, you are not growing; you're dying.

Now burning away the image, burning away the image. I say to you, *"Change!"*

"I'm afraid, I can't. I'd hurt so many people!" But you're dying! Change, you will find happiness.

"But I'll lose everything I have." You have nothing. Where is the genius that created, that can recreate it? They can take your gold and silver and your kingdom but they can never take the genius and the God within that made that reality, ever! They can slay your body; they will never slay you! You are eternal! It is the way it is! Change!

"I can't. People don't like me if I change." Change, entity, is what creation is all about. The creative process! Creation! It's not standing still and living the image. It is the metamorphosis. Stop being the worm! Be the butterfly! Now that's what your destiny is, is to evolve.

And the ancient schools were there to say, "Come here, come here. You're sick because the consciousness that created this experience is not the same, entity, consciousness that you have to have to resolve this experience. And the more it stays unresolved, the more problematic it becomes. And the more problematic it becomes, the more real it becomes. And the more real it becomes, it manifests in the body as disease. Now come here. Let's go back over what you're supposed to do. You seem to have forgotten it, eh?"

Consciousness and energy: the Gods, the light principle, consciously consuming subconscious mind creating new reality, changing, making a metamorphosis. What say you if you change? If you go to the unknown something bad will happen to you? Bad only exists if you create it in your reality. The unknown holds no "bads!" Remember, it is one vast nothing materially but all things potentially. The bad already smells; you've already created it. You move in energy to this next page in your book. You never, ever, ever, reexperience what you have owned as wisdom! There is nothing in the unknown subconscious mind that you have ever experienced! There's no hurt waiting there! There is no guilt waiting there! There is only life and all of its potentials. And it's your destiny to make it so.

"Then tell me — so I will feel better about myself — if I take this one step, what will happen? You're a God. You're supposed to know these things! I paid good money to come to this audience, to know what I am supposed to know!" Is there such a thing as bad money? How can I tell you what your unknown is? You have yet to create it. If I tell you, then I have created it. Do you understand?

You can only predict the predictable. To those who are in the rut, you can say the very hour of their demise and how they're going to die and what they're going to do next week and who they're going to run into and what kind of relationship they're going to go to. The rut looks like a piece of film and when you undo the circle and you see all of these frames and you hold it still, your life isn't moving. You see the beginning and the end. It's very predictable. It's those spaces in between the frames is where you should be going. That is subconscious mind.

Now this little scenario, needless to say, took a lot of drama, a lot of pain, a lot of vision, a lot of substance, to create as an actuality. And you're getting it in very rapid succession.

So here you are now with no ancient schools to run to because religion took care of that. Know you how many people died in two thousand years because of the God that was created? And all of the myths that their works are based on are snatches of truth from the ancient schools. Two hundred and fifty million people perished. And three quarters of that number were the people who were holding onto the fundamental truth of who and why they are here, not an insecure, psychotic God who kills his children because they do not serve him, because he's insecure.

So this ancient school is done very rapidly because you are living in a very rapid time flow now. And what I just told you, in this sort of packaged assortment here, took seven years to really understand, because here it doesn't do a lot to you. Some of you are still yawning and looking around — no true initiate would have ever done that — but you're getting it all. It is a lot in one fell swoop.

So we can go on to the reason that you are really here, that you think you are ready to know — and you're not — about the seventh seal. Because how can you know about this if you're sitting here with this identity crisis wondering whether you're really a man or a woman, and are you sitting here feeling insecure? Do you need to have a sandbox in which others can play and you can be the center of attraction? Do you have to be recognized for your wit, humor and sometimes genius? Do you have to imitate another person in order to be glorified? Aren't you good enough?

People who live here have no idea who they are; they are just the carnal image. Carnal doesn't mean decadent; it means everything connected with mass. This is your reality. If all you think about is how you look, you're never going to see the lights in the heavens! If all you worry about is your loins and your womb, how are you going to have the eyes to perceive a glory that walks by you or to see the light that is here on the stage, or to leave your body in a moment, or to elevate to the top of your roof? How are you going to do that, when all of your consciousness is thinking about who you are and what you are and your identity crisis — and your energy is making that a reality, and everyone in your life is a reflection of that reality — and all your thoughts are on that? You will never see anything because your reality hasn't grown to see it; that's the nature of reality. Why do some people see and others don't? Because they have not evolved to see! Their reality doesn't have room for it.

And every person in your life here is a reflection of who you are. You never see them; you only see what you are in them. They are mirrors to you, faceless mirrors, and they orbit around you. All of your realities are like bubbles and they're the same size and you're attached to one another, and when one moves, the other moves, and everyone looks like you. You don't see them, because if that person changes you cannot even identify with them; you have nothing in common. That is the term, is it not?

Now listen. What you think, you are. How you express, so is your life. You are only limited by your ignorance and refusal to see and to change.

Now in reality all of your problems you can solve because you made them and all they are is unrealized experiences. And what does it mean to be unrealized? It means that you haven't gleaned the wisdom from that experience that you pulled out of the unknown, and it sits there in your orbit as a problem, and it won't leave you alone. All it is saying to you is, "Please look at me. Tell me what I taught you. And if you can see that, I'll leave you alone!" And it does. It gives you up, and it is recorded in the book and the God is going, "Finally! Whew!" It says, "God help me, I try!"

Now all of these teachings were to move you. Look at where some of you have moved to; you live here. That was a physical move, but it was precipitated by a spiritual desire in consciousness to make it happen. It was precisely what you needed to do! That's just the way that it was. And for those of you that haven't, and something says, "Go for it!" inside, it's your image that's keeping you there and it's right here. The God is saying, "Move," or there may be others telling you, "You've got to move here," and this image inside is telling you, "You're not ready." Don't move; then you're impeccable, no matter what.

That is how you're supposed to live. Then you start writing in this book. You turn the page to the new you, a new page, a new beginning. Know what the new beginning is? You have closed the book on the past. Pages one, two and three are closed, and you should look at your past as being closed. You are not going to have a future as long as you live in your past. You are not going to evolve as long as you have not resolved your past. Your past doesn't exist. Where on the calendar does it exist? Hm? Where is the little girl and the little boy that played? Where are they? They are now; correct? Yes! Where are the past lives? Who cares? You are now and now is moving forward, and moving forward gets you out of the rut and starts you in the spiral of manifesting reality. Do you understand?

Every reality you manifest, your energy is traveling up these seals. This is the beginning of divinity, right here. It's not in your penis and it's not in your womb. It's right here, and that energy has traveled to this wonderful place. That is a person who is not the person they were yesterday, because they are ever-evolving, ever-increasing consciousness. The fire is moving; the Christ is certain. Did you understand?

What are the two principles? *(Consciousness and energy.)* And what

The Ancient Schools of Wisdom

do they create? *(Reality.)* Whose? *(Mine.)* Oh, you got it! Yes. So be it. Now what is the title of your book? *(Evolution.)* How many pages? *(Seven.)* It's a very short book!

Now this is where we begin this day's teachings, talking about these seals.

There are seven levels of vibration; there are seven levels of awareness. And we've just talked about the fall. In the Bible, in the religions, they talk about the fall of the spirits, that the evil ones were kicked out of nirvana, heaven, and they came to earth and the earth was their dominion, and they think they're evil. The truth is all of you came from the seventh, and the "fall of spirit" was the falling in vibration to make this journey. And that is not evil; that is hard.

So what about this brain that holds up your hairdos, or no hair? Every seal is opened by an action that is occurring up here. Now entities who are making this movement feel a swelling in their head, pain in their head — and if they don't feel it here, it begins to measure itself in their bodies — they can feel it. What that is is the pituitary — that sits between both parts of the brain — opening, and it blooms like a flower; it is called the blooming of the lotus. And from that, there is a hormone flow that begins to flow through the brain, that opens it up like magic.

And your brain, that is waiting like a flower, is there waiting to consciously consume the thought, the abstract coming from the subconscious mind, the Is. And it is abstract because it is unknown. No emotion is attached to it. It is a virgin, pure thought. And as you begin to work with this, that focus, that is a primeval alignment, that represents the triad or power within, comes right out here. That means the energy is now sitting here, and the focused brain, focused through consciousness, the God within you, is pulling out of that spiral the unknown and the next thought. It's called abstract movement. And the moment it happens, an electrical current begins to travel through the awakened brain — it makes a highway — and as it travels through there, something is happening. You know you are picking up something, but it isn't taking form, but it is coming. It's coming. Ever had that feeling? Welcome to the club!

And as it begins to make its trek — it goes through the spinal cord and it goes through the central nervous system — the entire body receives an electrical charge from this thought. And as it enters the soul, it begins to be held there — that's the reason for the soul — and contemplated upon, and all of a sudden an idealism is born in consciousness.

And the moment it takes form, the energy, as it is taking form, is heating up the body. It is a sure sign that energy is manifesting this conscious idealism. And energy begins to flow out of the body. It is now flowing through the levels of vibration to come to time that, in the next blurp on the spiral, is the realization — blurp! — of that thought. You just expanded your reality.

Now that energy that is created there, holds right here. "I'm hungry. The waters of life, of knowledge and of truth, that I hunger for." And the entity who is pulling consciously from subconscious mind has more than a reason to live! It has an appointment with destiny, to manifest and to realize what it's pulling up. Its light is growing broader on the darkness and this whole entity begins to be filled with feeling.

Now let's stop right there. That action is so pure — remember, the book is closed on the past — it begins to create a feeling here; it's called love. You don't do this here (first seal); you do it here (fourth seal). You don't love here; you love here. This is where it's born. This is where divinity is being earned, here, next to the thymus, the great, great fourth seal.

You begin to grow. And this wonderful heat that flows out of your hands is an energy that is given of grace and love, and it's powerful. And as that becomes the reality that is changing, the more one begins to create from the subconscious mind, the energy begins to move on up.

Now there is that which is called hydrogen. Know you hydrogen? When hydrogen changes, it changes into helium; yes? Then it is no longer hydrogen; it's only hydrogen potentially from the past. It is helium. When helium changes, it becomes lithium. What happened to helium? It changed. It's moving. It's changing. It isn't helium any longer. Its components don't even look like helium; it is lithium. And it all started from hydrogen. Do you all understand that?

Now you all start out as hydrogen, and you make an effort to be helium, but you end up hydrogen because hydrogen doesn't know it is going to turn into helium, and so it's scared for itself. Those who fear death live in the body, so it recoils; it's scared of the unknown. That is the image, because the image knows it will lay down and die in this life. And when it is threatened, a battle ensues, and the battle is the density of doubt. Moving through that density is the salvation of the transfiguration of who you are. So you're sitting there as hydrogen, and you want to know about the seventh seal. But once you get to number four it will never be three again. Hydrogen into helium into lithium. These are all your terms!

Now that is why movement from one area to another, the becoming process, is an arduous process because you have created it in your reality to be hard, and you've created in your consciousness that it's frightening and that you're losing self. You are — I want you to know — you are! Because hydrogen is not hydrogen anymore; it's helium. When you move this energy, that masculine identity image has to give up itself. It has to die in order to live. You must die in order to live again. And that is what it is to move this energy. You do die, and the old passes away and the new comes.

And when you come down to it, not a lot of you want that image to die, because you want to hold onto it. And you've got too much, done too much, to come as far as you've come. I understand that, but you're not willing to go to the next step, but some of you will, and eventually all of you will. But this is a bridge; this is what makes it happen.

I create my reality. I am its lawgiver and I have dominion over all that I perceive. When I got up off the rock, I couldn't get up off that rock until the humiliation of my people no longer caused me pain. To them, the immortal Ram had now become mortal. I was not larger than life any longer but small and hurting and injured. When I left the rock, Ram the barbarian had died, but the illumination of the entity was born, here.

Now this knowledge does this: It burns away ignorance, and ignorance is the mother to devotion, and devotion does not allow change; it allows only servitude.

Yes, you must die to live again. Your image must change by being burned away, that this imageless being can come forward. And you can never pretend that to happen because you cannot pretend an unknown; you have to be it.

You can pretend everything down here — power lets you do a world of material things — but you can't pretend to be up here, because this door is closed to the unknown. And the only thing that opens it is the God within who says, "This is where we make the big change." And this is where you're getting this pressing the most, and you can feel it, and you don't know why you're doing what you're doing, and no one says you're making any sense, but there is something going on within you. It is burning away the nonsense, to become this illuminated being that begins this journey of light in this spiral of time. And the glory of the one vast nothing begins to rush to this light and come into it. It is realizing and the light is growing and growing. Be a light to the world by being that which you are and all of your potentials.

You don't go here with an identity crisis. And you don't love yourself with an identity crisis. And you are not man and woman; you are God! You just are! And it is there where the forgiveness and the allowing and the grace and the love of you, to love yourself, begins! It isn't here (first seal); it's here (fourth seal)! And that's what allows you no longer to feel insecure!

Ten million people will not make you feel better about yourself! It is only that which is within you that can give you that! And you must go there and you must go there alone, trusting, knowing, feeling, embracing. And that's what makes all of these changes; that is what takes the caterpillar and brings forth the most beauteous butterfly, whose wonderful wings are like oriental fans and delicate, graceful legs, and only a flower is good enough for its presence. Get it?

Now *the dark night of the soul* is the chrysalis forming. And the emergence is a new person, a new being. Not a fanatic, but a new way of thinking, a new way of being. It's not what you wear or what you look like; it's what you are. It's not how you look that's going to save you! It's what you're made out of, that eternalness that you are!

So you turn, on page four, into the love of self. "From the Lord God of my being, give unto me." This is where you love yourself enough to know you're alive. And you're stretching that consciousness. And the quiet and the silence is necessary to hear, to be illuminated. And every day the lawgiver sits within its kingdom and knows precisely how to create this reality, that every word is not just a word; it is a commandment. Because you see, people, when you are in knowledge of what you are, you have shed a light into the corners of doubt and darkness, and you now are aware of what you're made out of, which means you have to take responsibility, which means there are no excuses. You can't say, "I forgot." You will never forget what you heard this day, never — it is too vital to you — so you can't plead ignorance. And what your consciousness now hears is growing, and what it grows into it manifests, and what you turn around and see is reality! You give it life!

And with everything that you experience, every word that you utter is a commandment to make it happen! Why can I look at you and send you a runner, just by doing this? What is it I own? I know I am God and you don't know that yet! You're moving to that place, to feel its power here. It's on page four; that's where it begins. It's the new you! You take control. You're not a victim, a whining, bawling, bitching, nagging victim; you are a master who speaks as a master. And it is not the tenuous that you are afraid of; you are in control of all the probabilities that float in you. I can send you a runner in doing this because you are the only thing that fills my consciousness in that moment, and that commandment is law. That's my reality and it isn't any other way. I don't send it and doubt it will happen. I left that long, long ago.

Now when I said to you, "Love what you are," I was endeavoring to break this away and move it up here. When I say to you, "Why are you so wrapped up in your sexual identity? Is that all that exists for you," I am ramming down your walls of reality to give you an option, because you don't see that option. All you see is this problem and, as long as you see it that way, it is going to be that way! If you see yourself impotent, you are! If you see yourself "overheated," you are! You just keep pushing those buttons. If you think you are a woman inside a man's body, you are! And if you think that's a problem, it always will be. If you don't think you're a good enough woman, you never will be. And if you can't satisfy your man, you're not worthy to. That's your conditioning.

I say to you, "There is more in you than this thing. There is more to what you are than what you can do. You are God! Change it! Become helium!" Just because you are born this way doesn't mean that's your destiny for the rest of your life. Every lifetime is the opportunity to own it all, because you create your reality. Stretch it, that you change, that these seals are closed forever and that this is coming alive.

This is the transfiguration of the Spirit. This is the hope. This is what is meant by being saved, by coming through the pain and the density of mass, to free up that great consciousness that can think of the beautiful prose underneath the weeping willow, or who finds a color of a fish in a babbling brook exquisite.

The Seventh Seal and the Garment of Light — Morning Session

Now how easy is it to make this transition, that is really the door that takes you to this one? It is as simple as you declare it; it is as hard as you know it, because everything is in your kingdom to regulate. Every time you look in that mirror of yours, what are you seeing? A few blotches, heavy beard, lice — we had them in my day, lice. If you see that every time you look in the mirror, you're seeing the image. How about looking in the mirror and seeing what you haven't seen? Something comes through those eyes and is talking to you, something that touches your arm, and it's this hand that touches the other hand, but this hand touches with such grace. There's something in this hand, there's an attitude in this hand, that that hand doesn't have; do you understand? We're making the imageless being visible instead of invisible.

Reality; you constitute it. You are it. Everything in your life is the reflection of your consciousness. You have to want to lay it down, peel it off, and be illuminated. You've got to want it not because it's the thing you should do today, or because your neighbor is doing it, or because someone said you should do it — don't you ever do what someone said you should do. You ask this first! You've got to want it. I wanted it. I was finished with all the expressions. I did not know that's what I was finished with, but I was finished with it; it was boring! You can only march so far and hack and beat and clip so much, where it all looks the same. You can only go so far; there's something else pressing. I wanted it.

You'll never pretend to have it; you'll have to change to get it. And you've got to want it enough to be it. You've got to want it more than judgment. You have to want it more than gossip. You have to want it more than malice and jealousy and envy. Don't you know that those who need the recognition are the potential enslavers? Don't you know those who have sat there are the gray men, they are the tyrants? Don't you know that they have not evolved? That is their evolution, their rut.

You've got to want to move! There's got to be something better! There is! Now we have a new reason to discuss the crowning seal, the crown of Christ.

Now want is what opens the chrysalis. And some of you will go through a raging fever. You'll think it's the flu and you will be sick, because all of the emotions in your reality are having to be burned away by the God within, who is burning the image. It manifests as a fever. And your consciousness is stretching and stretching, and every moment it is stretching, the movement of energy is occurring. And in this stretching there is nothing that is filled in there except the passion to move. Get it? Then you can walk away.

And, yes, there are things to do but they will get done. Not with sitting on your rear end, but with a light that knows how to manifest within your reality the ways to do it. It starts happening.

So here time is starting to go a little faster. Your manifestations start to happen very rapidly because you're not thinking, on the other hand, that you have a hard-on and what you have to do about that, or you're not thinking that you have a little passion down here, so you can't put up your food until you've taken care of this. It doesn't work that way.

It's here, and energy is focused and things are happening, manifestations are occurring. That spiral — the top blurp is matter/reality, the bottom of that spiral is antimatter/subconscious — magnetizes itself up as a design and becomes reality, and in the next movement it's becoming very quickly. And as you begin to live that, the next moment is the evolution of this energy beginning to move to this area. And this area is the commander. It is the great conqueror. It is a light that is ever-flowing. It is an entity who is aligned in absolute power, and the power is solidified.

And the energy begins to move to the sixth seal, and the sixth seal is simply a door to the seventh; it is the sacred door. You are reversing, back through mass, a spirit that has awakened the subconscious mind, and you are making mass into the vibrations of the seventh, so God is coming alive.

Ah, the master of the sixth. I have no words, in your words that are known, to tell you what that's like, only that those who are at the sixth seal do not allow dirt upon their countenance; it stays on the earth! They are entities who do not eat unless they want to, and they manifest bread by blowing on a seed, thrusting it into the earth, holding their hand on the ground, and the wheat comes. They are the magicians. And they can levitate from one place to another; they can rise in the sky. They can hold out their hands and all the birds within several miles will come to them. They are entities that can defy time, distance and space because they have collapsed the spiral.

How can you bless a seed, thrust it in the ground, and have the wheat grow in a moment, unless you have mastered time? And the only reason they mastered time is because they had the knowledge that filled the ignorance. They were aware, and what they're aware of, their reality becomes! Don't you understand? That's why you're getting a lot today. And they're the entities who, because they are collapsing time, can raise their vibration and go to the next dimension and do a ghost walk. They are the entities that don't have to travel in a ship to go to the other side of the sun but in a moment are there, because this is the only dimension with time. And they're there just because their reality says so; there are no gaps. And they are the entities that never grow old. Want the "Fountain of Eternal Youth?" Change! Yes! And they cease to grow old because they have collapsed time! Do you understand? This is the best I can do with your words.

And they of the sixth manifest in a moment, and they continue to call forth on the subconscious mind, and they have reached the exquisiteness of their potential. And when they can walk away from the gates of a great city, wanting for nothing, and leaving no tracks, they are crowned Christ. "My kingdom is not of this world for my kingdom is within me. It is not the garment that I wear. It is what I am. Love what is within you, for there is God."

And the Christ is one who has owned it all. It is the complete subconscious mind on fire in consciousness. It is all, the All, in one splendid human being, who loves not out of prejudice and bigotry, because love does not come from there, who loves because the life force, the principal cause, the principal Intelligence that is everything, is perceived by this being and this being is one with it.

It can sleep under a bridge and feel blessed to sleep there. It can eat of meager unleavened bread and feel blessed to eat it. It can walk into a barren desert and be blessed to be there, for it is relative and it responds according to the Christ, that is the awakened God made manifest in flesh and blood. That is the journey completed.

It is most ironic that they crowned Yeshua ben Joseph with a crown of thorns, because the great seventh seal — the pituitary in the brain — is wide open. It's bloomed like a great flower. The whole brain is alive. The road maps in the brain are multitudinous. It has facilitated that which is termed the unlimited mind and made it conscious completely. It is aglow! Why is there always a great halo painted above a Christ? Because it represents it is completely open! It is anointed!

But to crown this great glorious thing with a crown of thorns is very appropriate for his journey, and your journey, because the thorns of life are what it took to become that, and to have owned the pain, the humiliation, to have owned and been made rich by the troubles, to have walked naked and barely clothed and shamed not its body, to have looked into the eyes of all people and seen itself. How glorious. It was very appropriate because life is pain and it is suffering and it is not knowing and it is feeling helpless and, indeed, it is feeling deserted, and that God in that sky won't talk to you because it's not there; it's in here. That was an appropriate crown for a man realized in who he was in this life.

To the beginning.

When this (the pituitary) is opened and the final energy is achieved, the final destiny on the last page, one adorns oneself in a garment of illumination, a robe of light. And the robe of light is merely representative of mass that now has been transformed and goes back to the all-in-all, the giver of life, enriched, conscious, aware, that it merely transforms from this kingdom back to the highest frequency, light.

Listen, people, that old term "all is light" sounded swell, but the truth is everything is light, but it's a consciousness that has made it so. Everything here, it is created from light. A Christ has gone through the entire journey of this mass on that spiral, in that time flow, and has become the owner thereof and thus, at that moment, ascends — the transfiguration of the garment of light — back unto the highest frequency of all, light, and it owns all of the levels.

Now there comes an end of time — and there is coming an end of time — to where, behind the Christ, yesterday all rolls up as a scroll and it is gone. And in its place is a melody, a humming of memory, because the last page of the book of time has ended and it has completed a most remarkable journey. So be it.

You can't open the seventh seal with drugs or alcohol and you can't force it to bloom and you can't even pretend you are; you have to manifest it as an Is.

Now, my sweet people, like you that truth? Yes? It belongs to you. There was not one God; there was not one son. There is God within you and all are sons and daughters. There is not one Christ; there is, in the one vast nothing, all of your potentials to be that, that lies there waiting.

So the good news is you've got the knowledge. You take or leave

The Seventh Seal and the Garment of Light — Morning Session

it. If you take it, and if what I tell you is true, that you create the nature of reality, then now that you've been made aware that this belongs to you, it has to manifest, based on your choice. So be it! That's how you get on with it!

Now in the next seven years you have a destiny in the spiral of time, and the destiny has many doors and many options waiting for you; it has to. Everything you've heard here this day is an option created in reality, to go for it, as it were.

Now putting you on the floor and giving you a meditation, a little visualization, isn't going to do it, but that process makes everyone feel much better when they open their eyes. It makes them feel much better about who they are because the meditation was about hope and tranquility and sweetness, but it wears off after you get out the door. That was a reality that was created by a teacher and you all participated and, like magic, it works! That's only because the teacher is inducing you to choose that reality and, thus, you give yourself permission to do it, and so you create the aftereffect of it; do you understand? It works very well!

But there just aren't any teachers that tell you how to become Christ because they don't even understand to know it; there aren't any. There's no one on this level standing at the other end of the tunnel, and there's no one in the dimensions standing at the other end of the tunnel because no one has executed this knowledge.

You're going to be a lot of lanterns that now resonate a truth. And if you can spend those times meditating and you feel better, what would it be like to sit in an audience and to hear every word of an incredulous journey and give your permission to yourself to make it; will that not work? Yes? Yes, it does. I would rather have you have an appointment with destiny for the next seven years than to make you feel swell when you leave here and, like an aphrodisiac, have to come back to feel swell again. Do you understand?

Now I have desired to tell you as much as I could put into your lingo, your words, about this remarkable journey that only a few in your understanding have made, but whole civilizations have made it.

There have been no women ascend in your time-reckoning and in your civilizations. At the end of this epic, women will make their sojourn to Christ because someone told them the truth, that a superstitious God is only created by a superstitious person, and that God is not a man, is not a woman. God is consciousness and energy and the female expression is as divine as the male.

And when I address an audience like this, to pull out all the words that are understandable by its participants and its students, to keep your attention that you hear every word — because knowing that if you hear every word, you will experience them all — is the grandest gift I can give to you.

Now it was imperative to learn about how time works because when you know how it works, you will own it. It's likened as if you take a light and shine it into every dark corner, you will own its vision. And every time you have the light, you get rid of ignorance, a very enslaving consciousness. So enlightenment is not a ritual; it is an actualization of knowledge. And all you have to do is hear it because hearing it, consciously, enacts the energy to manifest it. Do you understand? Yes? And the more you can hear, the more darkness is taken away and the more enlightened you become.

Never say, "I don't know." Do you understand now why not to say that? Because if you say that, then you have ceased the opportunity of knowledge. Just say, "When I realize it, I will share it with you." Yes?

The seventh, sixth, and fifth levels are truly indescribable experiences. In one sense they've already been made sort of like the entity Superman; that is an appropriate image. And yet to give you this very small and pitiful description also begins the probability of its existence, and that is my achievement here. So I'm addressing your question in regards to "Can you tell me more?" I have told you enough to make it an experience that will manifest. The realization of that belongs entirely up to you.

No one in my time could even understand when I told them I went and flew like a bird above the camp. No one could understand that. And what you call it today is "getting out of your way to get out of your body." You can't get out of your body with an image; it has to be complete imagelessness. So I had no one to describe that to, but here I have an audience that is astute enough, that wants that, so I have done my best to engage you. And all of your experiences will be breathtaking, all of them!

And there is no fear, by the way, on the fourth page. Fear cannot exist unless it exists in the polarity of power. It is love. Hydrogen has become helium, and helium has become lithium. Power has become love, and love has become God awakened. Do you understand? So that is where you have been taken.

THE SEVENTH SEAL AND THE GARMENT OF LIGHT — MORNING SESSION

Now how do you do this in this real world? Yes, it does pose a bit of a problem. By changing your world, why must you be the victim of circumstance? Why not be the creator of it? And when you lay down the old and pick up the new, you are the creator of your world.

So why do you have to go home and feel guilty about being here? Recreate it. And if no one fits that image, it's time to change. Do you understand? That is that you "must die to be born again." You have to change how you think. You're not riding the rim of your reality; you're in the center creating it. And if the real world poses a problem, then get off of the rim of your reality and recreate that world as you know it, and don't stop until you have cleaned it all up.

Now that, of course, is the accusation from the "real world," to tell people to leave people and to break up families. Yeshua ben Joseph said, "Whosoever leave their parents and follow me, the kingdom of heaven is theirs;" and "me" being "a truth." And the truth is that in the Book of Evolution you have to turn the page. Do you understand? And your world, you should not be victimized by it; you should create it. Do you understand? Change it.

And don't go back and sit on your haunches and say, "Well, now I'm divine. I don't have to do anything." You're going to be more active than you ever were before and less hypnotized. Don't listen to the programming through radio waves and microwaves and the telly. Do not let it consume your mind; let the quiet consume it. It will energize you. Do you understand? Balance your life. You can laugh and have your party. Enjoy, but balance it with the need to listen. Do you understand?

And the trek home isn't really an unhappy experience. Freedom is a most exquisite joy. And freedom means, simply, not that you are free of your body, but it is a great mind that is creating. It's wonderful to give to another person just because you want to give to them, then you've burned away an image that says, "Well, now they have to give back to me." Do you understand? That's burning it away. It's wondrous to have grace in the midst of chaos. You've burned the yesterday away, and it is wonderful to see hope in despair.

Becoming is filled with joy. The people who have heard this message, that are called "Ramtha people," are the nicest and most joyful people in any despicable word called "sect" or movement there is; they are. And it makes me very happy, because I have not not noticed your wonderful deeds and their generosity — it has not gone unnoticed — and your smiles, and your brave heart, and crying when you see your food come up out of the ground and you know you're going to eat it — it's the best food you've ever eaten — and all your changes that you've made. And you don't have to be a drunkard or an addict to laugh and have mirth and merriment; it's just natural. It gets more so.

Loving one another is a result of loving yourself. Don't give and expect in return; just give. Do because it's there to do, to realize, to learn; then you're a great God, great. And, by God, if in all that you do, sweet and gentle lights and brave souls, no one notices, I have noticed — and one day you'll know how big "I Am" is! So be it — and an Is has expressed and it is now aware. So treasures are bountiful in this journey. Even through a crown of thorns, the pain, it has been worth it all.

Now in this journey you manifest no thing and regret it. There are no regrets on this path. Regret blows out the flame within; it is truth. Manifest to learn and be careful not to be caught in the illusion of experience. Do you understand?

In this school, this day is going to go on for seven years, and I'll be with you; I'm not going anyplace. And the changes are already in the throes; the gray men are doing their things and switching and now picking on other countries and changing their strategy a bit. That's all right; that's just what you want. That's what knowledge brings, the desire to make it different. You're getting your way.

Now in all that is coming, you're still going to learn. You have seven years of destiny awaiting. Everything I said here this day, I want you to live a sentence of it every day — and if you don't, a fortnight — so you can experience it and be enriched by it. And nothing is going to take you from me in these seven years. So be it.

THE SEVENTH SEAL AND THE COMPLETED GARMENT OF LIGHT

AFTERNOON SESSION

(As Ramtha enters the arena, the crowd applauds and applauds.)

I love you. I am very honored, most honored. I have no words.

*Ixt lahng actintu ahgdooglma.
Ihn mah Amaroosh ihn thah ag can dutheuhl sehmah,
ah lah uhm Amaroosh,
Ram.*

*From me to you,
I love that which you are.
From God to God
And soul to soul
And unto this journey,
I love all that you do.
So be it.
To life!*

Yes, I'm a barbarian, still! I'm happy you're here. This audience is growing! You are creating! Yes.

Did you contemplate what hear you this day? Did it make sense? It's called pure reason. Entities for eons have endeavored to keep you stagnated and ignorant. The ultimate intimidation is to say that the

The Ancient Schools of Wisdom

mind is the devil's workshop; that will stop you short from thinking on your own. It's coercion.

All you have to do is just take a person and say, "There's more to you than meets the eye," which is a truth, and press them to start thinking, stretch them to start experiencing, and they'll find such a wonderment and an awe and they will think they could never do all those things. They didn't know they could think that swell — or is it terrific? Terrific and swell! They didn't know they had it in them. They didn't know they could do that.

Well, the simplicity of these ancient wisdoms is that they are very simple. The simplicity is what set all of this into a rolling process. And pure reason is simplicity and it takes a simple mind to comprehend genius. It takes a simple mind to create wonders.

Now all of this teaching for ten years has really been to challenge and to bring down the complexities of what you think you are, because you think that the more complex you are, the more important you are. No, we are breaking down the complexities to see the shining simplicity, because it's only then that you know who you are: God.

"Well, it's astounding to say all I have to know is that it's consciousness and energy?" Yes.

"And that I really do create my own life?" Who else did?

"Well, that's true. And that all I have to do to change is to create that change in my consciousness?" Yes.

"And it will happen?" Yes.

"Can I change my mind?" Yes. It's all consciousness.

"So what you're telling me is that I don't have to be this way." That is correct.

"That I can be what I want to be?" You always were.

"These problems that I have, I really made them?" Yes.

"But they have all to do with money." I know, because you live to survive; you are not living to create. That's a whole different reality.

"You mean to tell me that I can do away with my past?" Yes.

"I haven't made any mistakes?" That is correct, for how can wisdom be a mistake?

"Hm. And God loves me?" You bet.

"Just by thinking it?" Yes.

"So what other things can I do?" As much as you're willing to perceive.

"So is what I perceive going to come true?" Truth is in the perception; reality is a result of truth.

"Oh. So tell me again, Ram, why I did all these things." Because you needed to.

"And I wasn't wrong?" No, you just got stuck.

"And it takes a higher consciousness to resolve the problems created by consciousness." Yes, that's all.

"Now you're sure I don't have to do anything special?" Not unless you want to; do you want to? Do you want more complexities? Would you like me to give you a chant, that if you chant it it is like a placebo; magically, it will make it happen? I can do that. You want me to give you this rock to wear around your neck that will somehow transform you into a master, and if you wear it you'll believe that you are? I can do that.

"No." Don't need that? "No."

"Well, what is this business about seals and stuff?" Don't make them a religion. Don't live for your seals; live to create. The seals open the energy and let it flow, and that process is called evolution.

"Oh. Is this truth?" Do you want it to be?

"Very much." Then it is. The saying that "there is nothing new under the sun" is a truth. What about over the sun? There's a lot to explore.

"Ram, you once said that I could dance with you in the sun, that it wasn't hot." That is correct.

"But then you said that the sun is hot. It is nature; it is violence." That is correct.

"Why did you say both things?" For they are both true! The sun is not hot and you can dance in its center, if that is your reality. But if your reality is educated in mass and that the thermonuclear furnace of the sun radiates heat that creates solar winds and radiation, if that is your truth, then it is. Do you understand? So both are held true.

"I see." Do see. Do look and see.

"Now, Master, can I just decide this day to do this?" Yes.

"Or can I go and think about it?" By all means, I do want you to think.

"How long do I have?" It depends on you.

"What do you mean it depends on me?" You have seven years.

"Oh! Seven years to make up my mind?" Yes.

"Oh. Well, what if I'm not ready to change? I mean, what if I like my reality? What if I'm comfortable right where I am? Nothing is sticking me and I've worked so hard to get here. Can't I still be enlightened and be here?" Yes, but your enlightenment is only going to be equal to your reality of comfort. You have your priorities turned around.

"How's that?" You want to be enlightened upon the basis of your reality of comfort. What created the comfort?

"No, you don't understand, Ram. Can't I just be God? I mean, does God have to be a pauper? Can I just be God and think it to myself and not really make a lot of problems? You don't understand, Ram, but there's a lot people out there that, well, I dare to say, don't believe a word of this, and, I must admit, I didn't either. But is it possible that I can just be like this and not tell anyone?" In that case you never have to worry because no one will ask, because people only inquire about something enlightening, and if you're a light, that's only when you're going to have to answer. And if they don't ask what makes you different, you ain't doing anything.

"Oh." Now to get back to your question. If your reality is that you are still controlling your kingdom, and if your life is filled with a lot of people who you don't want to share this with, then what are they representing to you in your life? What is their mirror? Is their mirror the lack that you have in yourself? Is it fear that they represent to you? Because they cannot be in your life and be that way unless they reflect what you are. And the best way to know if your reality is changing is by the reflections that are in your life, the people, power. What is going on in that reality you created? So what does that say about you? Are you only part a God, or are you all? Are you a duality? Are you a whore to social acceptance and a slave to enlightenment? Hm? People in your life are a wonderful opportunity to own the emptiness in your life.

Now what if everyone in your life is motivating, reflecting, uplifting, aspiring, inspiring? And those magnificent bubbles are allowing and living in freedom, and you're comfortable and happy? Then there is no reason why that kingdom cannot last until you are ready to say, "It is finished and it is of no importance. It is time to let someone else have it. Their turn has come to experience that; I am finished with it." That's when you move.

The Seventh Seal and the Garment of Light — Afternoon Session

Will you ever get to the seventh? You shouldn't live for the seventh seal. You should live for the opportunity to explore and to be all you can be in this life. And being all of that doesn't mean that you run around saying words that are mystical and magical and cause everyone to spin on their ear. It means being an illuminated soul, that those natural changes that occur in your life are going to occur naturally. You're not going to force the issue.

The more you concentrate on being celibate, the more passionate — or the word that you have, "horny" — you're going to become. It's a natural evolution. It is evolving and you just, one morning, know. It's not like someone came and delivered this message, that it was so shocking to you; you just know. And you know by your exquisite works, by your realizations, not by your laziness.

Now this little teaching, that the source will provide, where does that fit in with what you have just learned on creating? It's not an act; it's a process. And indeed you create for the process to create reality! So how can the source provide when you're not creating? How does the subconscious mind become your consciousness when you do not actively activate it? Those are lazy spiritualists, you know, those who won't dirty their hands with materialism, but they live like leeches off of everyone that is. That's not what we're learning this day.

It's not how much gold you put in your house; it's the genius that created it. That is the treasure, people! It's not what you painted on the canvas; it was the vision behind the canvas! It wasn't sitting there holding your hands to the sky! You're just going to collect bird droppings if you stay there long enough! Get it? Being spiritual isn't the path of the bum! It is the path of the innovator, the activity — actively pursuing. It's not what you make; it's that you made it. It's not that you have a job that pays you money; it's that you created it, people! The other is the aftereffect of actively pursuing and stretching consciousness. You're not going to get to the seventh on a credit card! You can't charge your way into infinity, putting it on "Galaxy Express;" just charge it! Well, it is the truth!

Every change — that you consciously expanded, then you manifested by activating it, and then you engaged it — you are making, changes your life based on nothing in the past. You only change into that which is the unknown, not the known. People in the groove do that; boring stuff! And it is changes done in the unknown that always challenge you to make it happen the next moment, that presses your mind. The seventh seal should be a carrot in front of your divine nose, that it inspires you to consciously pull up an abstract thought, embrace it, energize it, heat it, pull it forward into time, interact with it. Change, expanded reality, is like flexing and you're expanding, moving, moving, moving, that every moment demands the next, to be in control of; then you reach there.

But every adventure that you create is that essence that brings joy. Haven't you ever done something wonderful and knew that you've been happy about it, jazzed? And you feel slick and everyone says, "Congratulations," and pats you on the back and gives you one of those fixed smiles, and they don't know what it really is you're getting so excited about. They didn't think that was anything, but to you it was everything. So who was the most happy for you? (You) Yes! That is correct! Indeed! It will be that. Every accomplishment isn't a drag and shouldn't be a discipline; it is a process! That's where joy comes from, making something out of nothing — do you understand? — materializing out of the vast nothing potential. Now that's what this is all about.

Yes, you work, but it should be not because of the gold that it brings but what it is inspiring to the soul. What is it inspiring to the God? How much more wisdom have you gained from that experience; how richer are you in virtue? For every experience is coming here and then here and here and here, taking you home! Can you stay where you are and just change your attitude? Yes, but where you are will change; you must know that!

Does this have to be unhappy? No, unless you want it to be. Does it hurt to hurt people and disappoint them because you can no longer be what they want you to be? The only pain is that they cannot evolve to understand what you just did. If they could, there is no pain. Do you understand? The pain is not disappointment; it's their lack. You understand?

"Ram, am I really going to see those lights?" Yes. It's part of the process! Listen, people cannot see the quivering lights that are on other frequencies, that even if they lower the frequencies as low as I have lowered this one, they cannot see that because their reality has not stretched enough to pursue that. It isn't their reality. But a person who sees has stretched their reality to see it. It is common to them and natural. They are spiritual entities who see spiritual things. Now all things are Spirit; they just happen to see more than what you can see. That is a natural evolution of this process. Now I could tell you something, that it is part of the path that takes you to the seventh, because on the seventh you are Lord and have dominion over all dimensions, for you are the Lord God over them all and nothing is unknown to you. So the first inklings of those begin. And, yes, you will see. If you know that they are there to see, you will begin to see them, and they'll start out here at the side of you; that is the first process. And you're going to hear this hum in your ear, ringing; it's part of the sounds that go along with those lights. Yes, you're going to see them; it's natural.

And if you bless your trees and your earth, will it respond? Yes, because you had thought it was just dirt that had to be kicked around. But what if I said to you, if you look at it and say it is intelligence, that it will respond as an intelligent thing? What would it do then? It will respond.

What about healing yourselves? You're the sickest when you're the densest in your body. Did you know that? Because you manifest much more rapidly diseasements, and ailments and sicknesses and all of those things when you are the densest in the body. Consciousness and energy and this whole teaching will give you enough understanding that it will stretch your consciousness to take you out of that, and the body can be healed. It's not natural for the body to die; it truly isn't, especially to an enlightened being.

But as you evolve to what you have learned here this day and this appointment with destiny for the next seven years, you will find that you will have a decline in ailments and an incline in joy. So be it. Because sickness is as much a disease of ignorance as a mind that is devoid of reason. All you have to do is give it truth. That's it!

How can you evolve and be involved in an involvement? Evolution is an alone process. And you only need the herds because the herds in the beginning represent the mirrors to take a look at yourself, so you can identify that self exists. Yet when you reach this page, what is ironic is this is where the love begins and where the dependency is lost and it comes home to this, unconditional love. And aloneness; you are alone all of the way to the seventh seal. You bear that burden of density alone. For the God that you are is all that is necessary to make the journey. That is a truth; it's a lot less complicated.

"Well, how was your reality today?"

"Well, it's lagging behind."

"Want to talk about it? How is the pain that you're feeling today?"

"Better. But I still don't want you to go before me."

"I promised I wouldn't evolve faster than you could comprehend." Yes, I hear this a lot. "I'm not going to outgrow you, I promise."

Why don't you send them, instead of a greeting card, a sympathy card that says, "I'm sorry to hear you're not growing! You should be where I'm at. It's wonderful!" Yes, I make jest, but it's very serious because it involves things of the heart and, more importantly, needs of the soul on pages three and four, the endings and the beginnings: the ending of dependency and the beginning of understanding.

You can evolve together in a relationship, yes, but the individuals in the relationship do not represent one. They represent two individuals growing and evolving. One does not have to become small to feed the other, who becomes large; that is another game. This is equal to those who grow and experience, yes, and are always reflecting back to one another, because there is a shared intensity that occurs with individual experience. Oftentimes with the experience of one who is evolving at the same rate as you are, what you gain from their experience you can own as wisdom without getting dirty! That is a truth.

So what about your relationships, in lieu of what you have learned here? There is nothing that says you have to leave them to gain the seventh seal, but there's everything that says it's there for you to accomplish and you have to do it yourself. If you want company, wonderful. But you have to do it yourself.

Now what about your relationships? Remember, those people are in your life because they can only be there in that they represent a reflection of that which you are. So what are they teaching you? If they're hurting you a lot, do you feel you deserve pain? Are you the victim? And is that relationship a way in which to show you you're still unworthy because you have to hurt in order to gain affection, because that could be a reflection of yourself? And then if you decide that it is no longer what you wish, you'll have the courage to walk away because you have outgrown that experience and owned it as wisdom.

And can you go back to one who completely disbelieves but they say they love you? It's not important anyone believes this. Don't you know that belief is conjecture? There is nothing to guarantee that the unknown exists for you; you cannot prove that it exists, but you cannot disprove it either. It is a potential, a probability. And if you were to sum up the word hope, hope is the great vast nothing materially, all things potentially.

Is it important that a person believes? No, it's only important in their reflection to you, and that they are kind and loving and supporting. Is that not a God? Yes, it is. And they may not say the right words, but they're there and they have learned something called grace. When you are sitting there saying, "You've got to come and listen to this," and they're not budging but they're allowing you to come, they have learned something you haven't, the grace to allow. Do you understand? You have a wonderful reflection working in your life. And as long as that reflection can be seen for the beauty that it is, it will enrich the vision of what you are and help you bridge into this great seal, this place here, because it provides the friction.

But what about when one day you go home and you are tired of the battle? You know, "Well, you did this and you didn't consult me. I don't like what you did. You neglected me, this home, our appointments, our friends" — the need of the insecure to own through guilt. And if the guilt has been owned in you and there is not a need to play that game, you'll have to look upon them in complete understanding and say "I have owned this." And when you know you have owned it, the door in the next stretching of consciousness will manifest the next seal, the next dream, the next reality, pulled up from subconscious mind. Do you understand?

And love should not be a condition of who you are. You shouldn't love someone because they believe the same things you believe but because they're a reflection of who you are; it enriches them. They can be without any personal belief but have distinctive common courtesies — a gentleman, a lady — that reflects and enriches the partner. That is a blessing. You have earned them; they have earned you in their reality.

And last, what are you reflecting to them? You know, you see everything as a selfishness — which you should when learning to understand self — but when you get far out here you begin to see it all. And for your part, what are you giving the people in your life that are in your reality? What are you reflecting to them? If you are beginning to love what you are and you are beginning to find an impeccability living

THE ANCIENT SCHOOLS OF WISDOM

your truth, if you have found that it is no longer hard to keep from judging someone — you just don't do it — that you no longer have malice, and you're not plotting, and you're not teeter-tottering on the victimization that, "If you don't do this, then, well, this is all off," and what if you have grace and you don't need a lot to make you happy, it seems like life itself is just the joy of what you are. What are you to all those people, these friends, who obviously need a lot to make them happy? Could it be that you are the flame that's starting to flicker inside of them? Could it be they represent that? You are their flame, that little thread to something wonderful? Hm? "Is that how you do it?" Yes. I have been a wonderful reflection to all of you and I know it. When you know that about yourself to others, you have already owned and are finishing the writing on page four in the Book of Life. So be it!

Now are you getting this? Is this plain? Is it knowledge? Yes. Wonderful.

Now parents. I must tell you this all has to do with the seventh seal. And don't give me that guff you knew all of this, because you didn't. Parents, do you have parents? You have some? In the story of evolution and in the ancient wisdoms, when we choose to provide a genetic being, always the incoming entity hopes that the moment of conception is not conceived in passion but in love. There is a difference in conceiving a genetically-formed body in lust than there is in love. It changes the whole pattern of what will be selected from the gene pool of both parents. Now if it is conceived in love, you have a great God coming in, a great one. If it is conceived in lust, you have a troubled soul coming through. That's the way that it works.

Now when you chose to conceive, when the energies of both entities — no matter where you are in this state of evolution — conceive, copulate and through your love provide a body, you are drawing to you an immaculate being already evolved, who can come here and start teaching you at one year of age saying, "I know you. I was your mother. This is my mission. Sit down and I'll tell you about it. This is what we must do." Now that is the next wave that comes through in these last days.

But when you choose this, you only provide this genetic pattern, which they chose. They didn't choose you because of the way you look, but for what's in here. And they connect and they come through,

The Seventh Seal and the Garment of Light — Afternoon Session

and by the time the child is a year old they own it; they want to be it. You are simply a steward thereof of that energy. And if they don't know certain things, they're going to ask you and you're going to be impelled to teach them. And there are things they are going to teach you.

But you don't own your children. Your parents do not own you. In evolution, you are the body that is picked up and the character created for a drama to ensue that will enrich the experience of what needs to be completed on a certain page in the Book of Life. And everything you set in that drama, you want for it to occur just the way that it happens. When it is finished, when that is owned, the character is dissolved in the entity and the God comes through. That is the jewel that awaits every lifetime to happen.

But your parents are in essence the same light particum as you. They are your brethren and your sistren; they are to be loved. And if they could not love you, it is their lack that you can fill. But you love them unconditionally, for they have given you the door to continue this expression. For how else would you have come here? You're not at the seventh to materialize the body; you're moving through density. But after the drama is finished, this God has to come through. And it is as Yeshua said to his mother, "Woman, why do you weep? This is my destiny."

To your parents, you are not their child. They love you, for they have formed a stewardship for you, but you must do what you must do. That's why you're here. And you cannot live in guilt that you have not lived up to their dreams, their aspirations and their ideals because — think of this — that was only equal to their lack. You represented in their reality what they were not. You understand? You can't be that. You must move on. Love is always there. "Mother, why do you weep for me? Father, why say you I am wrong? For it is given to me the love to see you as you are, as I have never seen before." Do you understand?

What does this have to do with the seventh seal? Everything, because this is real life and this is understanding this process in real life, in the relationships in real life. It is wonderful to sit and be enlightened, to gaze upon tranquil waters when there is no friction. It's easy to say, "Behold God," but God is dead. It is God that is alive that is engaging in real life, that has to move through this density. It is not what life is going to do to you; it's what you're going to do to life! Do you understand?

And everyone in your life will represent your creation and be a challenge for you to say, "What did you teach me?" and then be humbled enough to own it. No, you don't have to go and say, "I was wrong," because how can wisdom be a wrong? Understand? Indeed? You go and say, "I have learned and I love, and I am grateful for who and what you are!" That is a soul that has opened its page that says, "Look at me."

Instead of saying, "You made me unhappy. You caused me to be this way. My parents did this and did that." Get off the victim stuff! That belongs down here. The God says, "Look at the opportunity I gained by having you as my parents," or not having any parents, because the true giver of life is within you that is the eternal Mother/Father principle. And you carry it within you.

Now what about your neighbors and your community? Don't live for your neighbors or your community. Create your neighbors and your community according to your reality. Do you understand? Be who you are and let this light burn! Don't put a cloth over it at night like you do your bird! Let it shine in the face of opposition, let it shine, because when they are opposing you, this God is saying, "What are they teaching you? What are you learning? What have you learned here?" And you'll learn it. Do you understand? And you're moving on. That's what this whole process is about.

And who is the true teacher? It's what's on the next page. It's what's in the next moment that you do this. And where is the courage? It is the courage to engage this and be it.

Now fears; fears are left behind here. They don't exist here because love does conquer all. Know you in my life the conquering of the Ram was that I conquered myself and every aspect of my ignorance. The greatest conquest will be the conquest of yourself and fear. What are you afraid of? Think you're going to die tomorrow? So what? To you that's a big deal, eh? But you live in fear so much that you create the reality of accidents. Because if you live in fear you create its polarity as a reality; there is always going to be someone hiding behind the door or under the bed. Do you understand? And if you think Spirit holds evil forces, then you dare not go into the unknown because it's going to get you — and it will and no one is going to believe you; that's the terrible thing. It's truth. It's a true story. So what are you going to do?

The Seventh Seal and the Garment of Light — Afternoon Session

Afraid; if you picked up this body in this lifetime and you've laid it down millions of lifetimes, why are you worried about dying? Only the image cringes at that word because the image is that face, that hair, and that body that goes into that box, that hopefully is preserved, that won't go to the worm. Do you understand? And that's what you can't imagine. But this is eternal. What do you look like? You're a brilliant light, a light that is emanating power. It is indeed awesome.

Now my runners to those that attended that which is termed Reality, was to send them a view of their Spirit. And it is very difficult to do because how is the Spirit going to create itself to look at itself? But their runner is exactly that. And they are going to see this entity stretched way out in front of them, this being of light. That's all they'll be able to see. And it wasn't really a visible face; it was a presence, and it was there standing in the doorway. "But I felt connected to it!" You should; it's you! It pulls you right from here (fourth seal) and it stands there saying, "It's me. This is what we look like. Disappointed?" And if you have infrared film in your camera and you said, "Hold it," you will see this blob of energy standing there. "It's wonderful! But it posed! It went along!" It's all right; it's hip! Now that is the essence they have photographed of entities at the moment of death, that they see this essence leaving. That's what we're talking about here.

And you know, only the image is afraid. The God inside takes marvelous journeys. It waits to do that. This is you and it is eternal, and it becomes very detached when it moves out of the body upon death. It doesn't feel like it should come back to it. You try to save it; you cut it open, you're pumping it, you're sticking tubes down its throat, you're stabbing it, and this thing is going "beep, beep, beep," and they've slapped this thing on your face, and they've ripped your clothes off! And they're doing this! And the body is just there and the Spirit is trying to burst out, and everyone who runs around in their images is trying desperately to keep it from going anywhere. "It's going to come right back here and be who I want it to be!" And the images that call for it are all of those people who, in their reality, are the doctors and the nurses and the anesthesiologist, the urologist, everyone! And it is their stroke to make you live. That's their reality; they saved you. And then you have the family out in the hall and they cannot afford to let you leave! Do you understand? It's a heavy decision.

And so the imageless God, the Spirit, is going, "Oh, give me a break! It is so much nicer here. Why can't they just see that it is nicer here?" And so everyone is praying for God to bring you back. And it stands there and it listens to all of the prayers, the sorrows and the wailings. And even that person — you don't even know why they're there — is there praying for you. They never were when you were around! You don't understand this! And so they're asking, praying for your life! What can you do? So you make the choice to come back. You barely remember something going on, but something pulled you back, but you wanted to go. That's what it's like. So the thing that holds you is the image. "I've got to have you in my life. God, you can't leave me. I love you. You just can't go! You're my rock!" Do you understand?

Fear; underlying death is fear. And death represents the unknown, and the unknown to the image represents being out of control; you can't control it. Do you understand? So when you turn it around, you're thinking, are you going to lose all of the people in your life because you've become strange? Yes, that's a fear because that means the image doesn't have anyone to relate to, it can't see itself any longer and everyone is mad at it. It wants to try to do something, to put back the mirror so it can talk to itself; do you understand? It's how it works. And if you're afraid that someone isn't going to love you, your lover or your husbandman or your wife, because you're different, are you going to not move forward because you're afraid you won't ever find anyone to love you again? No.

Listen. This is a borrowed body; it's on lease for a purpose. But this isn't your body; it belongs to someone else. And you can't lift me around like a doll and take me anyplace you want to. What you love about the Ram is what you can't see, and that's the God, the Spirit. And look how many love that which I am. What have I lost to gain you? What have I lost to gain eternity? And yet if none of you be in this room, I am still lifted. You understand?

Fear is the guardian to the door that shuts off consciousness from pursuing subconsciousness. You are afraid to be alone and you're afraid to be quiet. Your natural urge is to turn tunes on or static on or entertainment on, because you're afraid to hear what you're going to think. You're afraid to know about yourself. You're afraid to confront yourself. So all of these things are excuses as why not to have to do that. But in the quiet is where you find this, this love, that enables you one day to stand and be at peace in the midst of chaos.

And, people, what if the whole world despised you, they hated you, because you have moved out of the status quo? You didn't want war anymore, you couldn't fight; what is there to fight? The conquest is with oneself, not with one's brothers. And what if you didn't want to pay monies to the munitions dealers who keep war going?

And what if you said, "I don't want to look like the ideal woman. I already am." And what if you said, "I am a man, but it has nothing to do with the size of my penis, or how much hair I have on my chest, or how many sons I sired, or how much money I have in my pocket!" What if the world hates you because you love the earth and you weep when the dolphins die, and your heart heaves when the great trees, the old gentlemen, are dying because poison is raining on their heads, suffocating their beings? And how much trash can you make? How civilized are you, that you can't find a place to put your civilized byproducts that does not corrupt the natural flow? Is that civilization?

And how many things, the ones you eat that have containers — yes! They emit gas, yes — because it's cheap and it's convenient and you can throw it away. Where's it going to go? What if the world doesn't like you because you say, "No! Give it to me on my hand! I'm not going to throw them away! That's what they were made for! I have the best utensils in the world right here." And you consume it and the only by-product is the dung and it is biodegradable back to the earth, but there's nothing to throw away. And what if you say, "I will not eat any more of these burgers because it was made with the meat that the forests were cut down for, to raise the meat so they could be cheap for me to buy," and the great forest will not come again until the earth rotates on its axis. What if the world hates you for that? And you say, "No!"

And you love when people want you to hate, and you're a peacemaker, a righteous person — the "right use" in consciousness. What if the whole world hates and says to you, "Silly buffoon, how could you listen to something so incredulous?" And then look at their life; what are their demons? Man, who says it does not believe in the existence beyond death, will die, for that is his reality. A woman, who says this does not exist, will always be a slave to being a soulless being.

And if you can make a stand — even if it is to sleep in the boughs of a great tree and that is the only place you can and you do — and own this truth, then you have become a flame in the wind, eternal.

Then that has opened up the fifth seal for the master's walk. Because when your reality no longer is consistent with what you have left behind, then the unknown is your reality and it is only there that unbelievable things can happen. They do not happen in social consciousness; do you understand? Social consciousness does not have the reality of antigravity! It is a trashed society! It throws away people as easy as it throws away its paper.

It's only there in the fifth that you begin to open this part of the brain that allows you to defy everything that is status quo, all physics and all sciences unifying consciousness, unifying fields. That's when the master is born, because you have to close down all of that and own it all before you can stand naked in the probabilities of the one vast nothing but everything potentially.

You want to levitate? You want to get out of your body? You want to travel through time dimensions? You want to talk to the people from the other side of the sun? That lies in the fifth seal, that has moved from the fourth, and that is when you have owned all of this and your only reality is what is in front of you and that's it!

Then you move on to a Christ who can pity the world, who can love the world, that the idealism of what you've become is the hope of every human being there is! It is the hope of the people who are starving in the streets! They started out starving because that's an experience to press them to create, and they got lost in the experience! They don't even know how to take care of themselves! They are lost in the pain! And the homeless are out in the streets, indeed, in your cities, like a disease. And the socialites turn their heads and cover their noses with silken hankies to get rid of the stench and pretend they don't exist! And politically they don't; they're thrown-away people. And they became homeless because that was their choice! But it was the opportunity to move through it, to get out of the rat race, not becoming a rat. Get it? There is a lot more to becoming than just saying, "I am becoming." There is a lot more to saying, "Behold God" than just saying it. It is being it.

I've taken you through the things you've created: your sexual problems, your dis-easements, your identity problems, your rich, your poverty, your investments, the rise and fall, the unpredictability of other people's wills and living off someone else, all the way to getting rid of all of it, owning it so you could come to sovereignty, where true freedom exists! Do you know there are entities who live the whole day to watch the stock market? Their whole day is lived watching it! What are they going to do when it does something? Do you understand?

Well, I wanted to say these things to you. To be righteous you have to want to, and only righteousness takes you home. You want all the miracles but you don't want to do anything to create them. You want someone else to create them for you — they'll never happen; it was you — and it's learning how to be that.

I wanted to say to you, God, I know you've had pain, but it is from pain that you grow. And I know it's been hard and you've been humiliated and spat upon and talked about and laughed about. And I know it has been hard to hold your head high and at times it has been difficult to find even a friend that you could trust. I know that; don't you think I have watched? But out of every incident, it forces you to create.

Someone told you a long time ago, "Stop thinking; it's the devil's workshop," but, I say to you, it is with reason that your natural urge is to create, and every incident that you've had has been a grand opportunity to create! If someone has given you the money that you needed, it is a manifestation of need! Be thankful and be honored! If the door has opened, it has opened! You have created it!

But you must die in order to be reborn! In order to come again, you must die in one consciousness to engage another! And it has been hard, yes, because you're called a cult — which has turned out to be an insidious, hideous name — but all religions started out as cults. This is not a religion, but it is called that to insinuate something that is bad, nasty, ugly, and baffoonish.

God is not insecure; it is what you are. The kingdom of heaven is within you; it becomes a created reality outside of you. And hope in this truth is everlasting life, a glorification that the coming of Christ is that which is within me, to be realized on the seventh. I'll meet you there.

And it is not your lot to die by the bomb or polluted waters or rain or the splitting apart of the earth in its cataclysms; it is your lot to survive. The grandest thing about you is evil doesn't exist in you. So be it.

nough. Everyone of you that are in the audience came because I called you to be here, and everyone of you who ever came in all of these years came because I wanted you there.

You've been contacted and you were chosen long ago, long, long ago; it's in your book. And I'm so pleased you listened to this incredulous thing that is happening in front of you, but it is what is going to change the world. So feel special and feel loved; you are. And look at tomorrow as the day and look upon every moment as the opportunity to live, that everything you do, you create. And that in this life, and at the end of it, won't be a crown of thorns but a light. That's what I want for all of you.

And you've created your realities and you can see so clearly how you have. And that no one has been pulling your string; you've been at the helm of your ship all along. And that if all of those things came to pass like they did and all the things you heard this day are waiting to be realized, then they are just as real as everything else you have done.

Now the moment of glorification is the moment that, in the consumption of life, you have achieved and mastered and owned all of its parts of possibilities. And that is your divine heritage. That belongs to every single one of you, not to one person but to you all.

When I said I came here on my father's business, it's your mother's business as well because evolution is cosmic big business, and this big business is going on. I want you to know and to realize that you, my precious people, are going to deserve everything that you experience and evolve to. You're not going to have any more runners from your past. We're going to close that book — so be it — because you cannot have the knowledge of the seventh and keep looking backwards, so we close that book. And no runners will come from this house to you again pertinent to your past, for all of the runners that are coming are pertinent to the spiral of matter, that are coming from subconscious mind, and they are all adventurous. So be it.

This has been a wonderful audience, inasmuch as I have kept my word about most of your runners. There are some of you who said no, and they've all locked up at your door waiting for you to open it up! For what I said, there is a truth; so shall this be. I cannot control the will of man or the gray men, and I can't tell you the moment nature takes its dip into antimatter. All I can say is that it is its evolution and it is on the moment, any moment. I can tell you of conspiracies, but until they've ripened in the moment, no one knows; just that they exist. But I can tell you what I can do, and from this day forward in the next ten years, all that comes to you is coming from the unknown, rather than the known. And you have earned that and it is my privilege.

The Seventh Seal and the Garment of Light — Afternoon Session

To fireworks!

Yes. Now there are those of you who are making your trek to the mountains and there are those of you who could not come. Do not be disheartened, for you came these days and these are the most powerful teachings; the rendering in the mountains will have to do with fire. But those of you who do not come, I will work with you in the same premise. You already have an appointment for seven years of learning; your destiny is already set in the time flow. I will continue to work with you. It does not mean that you are not loved and that you won't be missed. To them, you will be; you're not missed to me. Yes.

So there is a march ahead, and there are also new mountain ranges getting ready to be born and new continents waiting to come and the old to pass away, there are comets waiting to enter, there are bellyaches in the crust that are ready to move, there are many things setting in the stages and in the hangers; that is natural evolution. It is dying that it can live again. The earth is preparing to rebirth itself as the birth of a phoenix. In ten years, as you call it in your time and counting, many turbulent things will begin to occur — they're already working — but you have a destiny and a path. Every step of the way will be on solid ground because there is something that must be achieved. And no matter what happens, you're going to learn that. So do not react in fear; react in anticipation, because change is a blessed thing. So be it.

You have learned? Yes? What are the two principles? *(Consciousness and energy.)*
What do they create? *(The nature of reality.)*
And what is that? *(Life.)*
Whose life? *(Mine.)* Are you sure it isn't your wife's?
And what is wisdom gleaned from? *(Experience.)*
And what creates experience? Oh, come on! Who creates the experience? *(I do.)*
From what? *(Consciousness and energy.)* Correct.
And what do you create? Something you've done before? *(No!)*
And what is unknown mind? *(God.)*
And what is the destiny of consciousness? The destiny of consciousness is to make known the unknown. Got it?
And what is the unknown? What is it? See, you're being tested already!

167

The Ancient Schools of Wisdom

Now what do you create a problem with? A problem is an unrealized wisdom from an experience, and the consciousness that created the experience is not the same consciousness that resolves it! *(Right.)* Right, yes! That's right; you got it!

This is important for you because there's a lot of you that wear your problems like emblems of sorrow and that you can't get beyond them! But don't you understand that you have to look at them and say, "What are you teaching me? What have I learned here?" And the moment you understand its learning, it gives you up and becomes wisdom! And that is superconsciousness that does that; get it?

Now the same consciousness that just resolved that into wisdom, is that the same consciousness that pulls an abstract from subconscious mind? *(Yes.)* No, you have to stretch your consciousness to pull up abstract thought from subconscious mind; do you understand?

And what is God? *(I am.)* Yes, you are. And if someone has a problem with that, it's their problem; do you understand?

Where is the kingdom of heaven? *(Within.)*

Why would it be within? Because reality is created by conscious intrusion into subconscious mind. And the truth is you can have whatever you want; you just have to conceive it in consciousness. Is that not a kingdom? Yes.

How many seals are there? *(Seven.)* Where are you? *(Fourth!)* I appreciate your honesty.

What is the purpose of the seals? Think! You all can talk because I'll hear you all. It doesn't make any difference how loud, but explain it; I want you to explain it. If you can, you will own this truth! *(Jumbled mass of different answers.)* Yes, that is correct!

Now there is a religion, based on my old peoples, called "chakra" and it begins on the floor. The truth is, it doesn't happen on the floor; it starts right here (first seal). This is where all the fireworks go off. Your feet have nothing to do with it. Now that is different than these seals; this is the way home through mass.

Now who created the seven levels? *(I did.)* Did they exist before? *(No.)* Are they still there? *(Yes.)*

How are they represented? *(The seven seals.)* That is correct; by the seven seals, in consciousness.

And what is the seventh? *(Christ, God I am.)* What is it? Say it. *(Christ.)*

Christ. And what is that? *(Fully realized.)* Yes, and realization is a matter of reality, isn't it? And a matter of reality is the result of what? Consciousness and energy.

What does time look like? *(Spiral.)*

What is the opposite of matter? *(Antimatter.)*

What is the opposite of consciousness *(Subconsciousness.)*

And what is subconsciousness? And what is consciousness? Yes. It is the awakened unknown. So be it.

Now is there anything in your life that cannot change? *(No.)* That is correct.

And your life is a collection of who? *(Reflections, bubbles.)* That is correct.

How did all those bubbles get attached to you? *(My creation.)* How did you get attached to them? *(My creation.)* It's a little humbling for someone to say, "But I created you."

And you say, "No, you didn't! I created you!"

"You couldn't have!"

"No, I created you in my awareness."

"Well, I wanted you to be here. You're here because I said yes! Remember? I went out with you, remember?" Someone else can create you in their reality; all you are is a reflection of self. Correct?

Can you be happy? *(Yes.)* How?

Can you be unhappy? *(YES!)* Oh, listen to this! Yes! You owned that!

What is home? *(Seventh.)*

What is the image? *(Antichrist.)* Yes it is; the image is the Antichrist because in order to become, you must burn it away. It is what you lay down. It is the caterpillar that comes from the chrysalis as the butterfly. It is what you must own. Your image cannot be your priority in your life; it must be you that is unseen in the creative mind doing something. Creation is a process; it is not an act.

Do you choose? *(Yes.)* Do you create only one choice or many for you? *(Many.)* Yes, you do. Because there are people in this audience sitting here who have closed down their opportunities by only creating one way, and are not being able to live up to that one way. Don't you know why people die or take their lives? Because their consciousness has collapsed because they have not given themselves choices. Choices are a matter of creation. And the ultimate destiny is to be all you can be.

Can you predict the unknown? *(No.)* No, you can't. So if you cannot predict the unknown, then it becomes the purest adventure there is.

And last, do you love that which you are? *(Yes.)* The hardest thing for a man to say is he loves himself. But that's his mastery.

And change, is it necessary? *(Yes.)* Yes, it is. So when you change your mind, is that your right? *(Yes.)* It's your destiny.

And did you ever make a mistake? *(No.)* If you want to get rid of some people in your life, tell them you never made a mistake. It will blow them off quicker than anything! You haven't.

Now the seventh seal is actually a gland, but it is also the electromagnetic field that happens as a result of that gland blooming — it is the mysterious, strange pituitary gland — because it is really the physical key that allows the brain to begin to open to greater realization.

Well, a lot of people have called that their third eye. "Well, my third eye clicked on and I could see all of this." Get out of this space! Your third eye doesn't exist — unless you want it to exist and, of course, it will be there — but it is awareness. It is the brain being activated to be able to entertain an abstract thought to start creating. A very active mind won't leave you alone. It's moving all of the time. All of those moments you hear it going on and on and on, it's expanding. And those headaches are from that gland opening. Now that only happens when you have knowledge that tells you what it is and what it will do. That will give you the courage to say, "I want that" and be willing to live it. It begins to physically open and allow your body to change.

The seventh seal is here because all of this has been activated, to be able to live long enough to own all of the possibilities in this sleeping brain mass. It is patterned precisely with the adventures in the unknown because you have to have something to pull from in order to activate this, to utilize it. A genius, or what you would called an illuminated being, has gone to the capacity of physical mass, which means they have gone to the capacity and have opened completely the seventh seal. That is an illuminated being.

Every moment that you engage and every moment you laugh and every moment that you feel and every moment you can be quiet and let this work and listen to what's going on in your head, every moment you engage the subconscious mind, you're growing. It's opening. It's working. You are creating. You're moving. Laughter moves energy.

And the Kundalini sits at the base of the spine that's supposed to rise up — a serpent that's coiled to come up — and it opens all of this stuff. It isn't at the base of your spine; it's the energy flowing through these seals. That's actually the tunnel you go through when you die. It comes out the top of your head; that's the end of the tunnel. This energy that's moving doesn't just come up and bang and go back down. It doesn't work that way. And that was some person's creation for the excuse as to why they couldn't stay the way they were. So that's a myth that's been created.

The point is when you start to move energy, you don't go back. It just keeps coming. And you can stop anywhere that you want to along the way, a whole lifetime! That's all right. As long as in that place, and in that seal where that energy is coming from, that you continue to live — you can't stop living — but every step of the way is engaging this up here. And the seventh says you have evolved all of it in mass, all the capacity of mass, to realize. And that's when it is finished here and you leave no tracks. And you're gone; you belong to eternity.

So every time you laugh and every time that you have a wonderful thought and every moment you move through the density of doubt with joy, and every morning you wake up and you do this to the glory of life, every moment that you can voice, in your own words, what it is you're knowing, it's opening. And every moment that you live your truth, because that is what you want to live, you are living righteously. And every homeless person, you look them in the eyes. Don't turn away but look at them because it may be that look and that love and that God that awakens their flame. Do you understand? Because everything that you perceive becomes reality, everything you touch becomes alive, and everywhere that you see God it will respond. Do you understand? And every moment you say you love that which you are, this is blooming. And every moment that you move out of your shadows and shine the light in there, you are growing. Do you understand? And every moment you love, you grow.

I have been a great mirror to you — and some of you have never wavered from your first audience; you've been constant — and every reflection was to take you home. Every moment was to say, "Come, I want to talk to you. I want to enlighten you. I want to explain to you. You're ready for me to tell you things without you becoming afraid. Now you can learn." I'm waiting at the end of this life, and at the end of these experiences, so you have your ideal; an ideal, something you can't even see; you just know it and you feel it. That is God. And you have not wavered all the way through.

I was honored to tell you these things because if I would have given you all of the gold in the world, it would have been nothing compared to the treasure of these days together and what I was able to say to you. Because when it comes from my reality, it is absolute and it gives you a fighting chance in all that's coming.

So to the glory of the Christ within you is a truth and to what you can achieve. Don't deny yourself its possibilities by throwing it away. Own it every step of the way, and you have to only own what you feel you are capable of doing, little by little by little. Do you understand? And I'm with you all of the way. We started something here and we're going to finish it! So be it.

I would like to stay much longer with you in this body, much longer, but there is coming a day to where I don't have to show you in this body because that's all you can see. You'll be able to see this light and come and listen to this audience from a light being. So be it.

(Audience applauds for a long time.)

Yes! Yes. One more toast, and we're off to some adventures.

From the Lord God of my Being,
I am.
And unto my world I create,
It shall be of harmony
And of love,
Of grace,
And of light.
Be of my world,
For there is the comforter,
The Lord God of my Being.
So be it!

This audience is over.

I'll see you in the mountains and, the rest of you, in the wind. You have learned splendidly. So be it! Yes!

P.S.: This evening and tomorrow morning I wish to look upon your face as you are contemplating, in consciousness and energy, to begin to change your world, for I want you to see the miracles that you can do. So get on with it!

OTHER RAMTHA TITLES

The following is a list of books on Ramtha available through RSE Products and Services and other fine book stores. Also available is a whole library of recordings of Ramtha's teachings. All products are available through mail order at:

RSE Products and Services
PO Box 519
Yelm, WA 98597
(360) 458-4771 or (360) 458-2956
email: greg@ramtha.com
Website: http://www.ramtha.com

✤ **RAMTHA** *Edited by Dr. Stephen Lee Weinberg (217 pages)* The classic work on Ramtha, that Ramtha himself has referred to as "The Great White Book." A brilliant book designed to inform the general public as to the nature of Ramtha's teachings along with a rich sampling of his wisdom on many topics. Highly recommended for those ready to understand this great teacher and his message. It is one of the most important books to read if you are preparing to enter the school.
#1401 - Hard Cover $ 19.95
#1401 - Leather Bound Edition $29.95

✤ **RAMTHA: AN INTRODUCTION** *Edited by Steven Lee Weinberg, Ph.D. (228 pages)*. An engaging collection of teachings that will appeal equally to those familiar or unfamiliar with Ramtha. More than an introduction; a true treasure of personal mastery.
#1404 - Soft Cover $ 9.95

✤ **LOVE YOURSELF INTO LIFE** *Edited by Steven Lee Wein-berg, Ph.D.* All who enjoy Ramtha's profound and eloquent teachings will cherish this comprehensive collection of work on a wide variety of topics culled from Ramtha's exchanges with people. Almost 500 pages. Destined to be a collector's item.
#1405 - Large Soft Cover Format $ 39.00

✤ **I AM RAMTHA** *Edited by Richard Cohn, Cindy Cohn, and Greg Simmons. (127 pages)*. This book is a beautifully photographed book that accompanies thirteen of Ramtha's most universal teachings. Wonderful teachings on the subject of feelings, being at one with nature, unconditional love, and the prize that is called life.
#1201 - Hard Cover $ 9.95

✴ I AM RAMTHA   *Edited by Richard Cohn, Cindy Cohn, and Greg Simmons. (127 pages).* Signed, Limited Collector's Edition No two alike. Each cover individually made with a combination of hibiscus, Hawaiian native herbs and 24K gold flake. The paper is handmade and the photos hand-selected. The spine is parchment and the book is bound by a man trained in the rare book section of the Vatican Library. A timeless treasure.
#1201-A - Special Order Only $ 99.50

✴ A STATE OF MIND   *JZ Knight. (445 pages).* The intimate account of JZ's life in her own words. Her story, which includes her humorous and poignant introduction to Ramtha, is a story of the triumph of the human spirit. Also available in an edited audio version, recorded in her own voice *(120 minutes)*
#1501 - Hard Cover $ 9.95
#1501.1 - Cassette $ 9.95

✴ TO LIFE!   *Compiled by Diane Munoz.* At the beginning of each audience, Ramtha elegantly and thought-provokingly salutes the God within with a toast. This book is a selection of the toasts from Ramtha's audiences from May of 1988 through May 1996. A wonderful way to start your day.
Soft Cover $ 15.95

✴ THE SPINNER OF TALES *Compiled by Deborah Kerins. (228 pages).* Ramtha has captivated audiences throughout the years with the telling of his tales. Now they have been put together in book form to be preserved and delight readers of all ages. These stories are from the earliest years of the teachings to the most recent. A true treasure! (#1 Book of 1991)
#1300 - Soft Cover $ 10.00

✴ THE LAST WALTZ OF THE TYRANTS   *Edited by Judi Pope Koteen. (153 pages).* This book is a synthesis of Ramtha's teachings on the challenges we face by those who control the world economy and from the coming radical changes in nature. It provides inspiration and practical guidelines to enable you to be prepared.
#1202 - Soft Cover $ 11.00

✴ UFO'S AND THE NATURE OF REALITY: UNDERSTANDING ALIEN CONSCIOUSNESS AND INTERDIMENSIONAL MIND   *Edited by Judi Pope Koteen. (221 pages).* This book is a sometimes shocking, sometimes comforting picture of what we would call alien intervention in our history, in our present, and in our future. It allows us to see what is "out there." But this

is more than another UFO book. It exposes the limitations of subjective mind and encourages the reader to move into inter dimensional mind, the source from which all is available. This book will alter the way you've perceived everything you've been told.
#1611 - Soft Cover $ 11.00

✤ CHANGE: THE DAYS TO COME *Ramtha (149 pages)*. Based on the 3 day intensive taught in Denver, May 1986. This book tells of man's destruction of Earth's resources and nature's recourse to heal herself. This book has never been more timely than the coming year.
Soft Cover $ 10.00

✤ SOULMATES: THE INTENSIVE *Ramtha. (128 pages)*. Based on the 3 day intensive taught by Ramtha in Seattle, WA, January 1986. This book spells out the mystery of the science of soulmates and its importance in the knowing and loving of self.
#1403 - Soft Cover $ 10.00

✤ BECOMING *Edited by Khit Harding.* The second Ramtha book, now a classic of which there is a limited supply. A non-linear teaching on the becoming process
#1101 - Soft Cover $ 14.95

✤ MANIFESTING: A MASTER'S MANUAL *Edited by Khit Harding. (100 pages)*. Based on the November 1986 intensive, The Power To Manifest, this is compiled such that each page serves as a thought-provoking concept for contemplation and understanding.
#1102 - Soft Cover $ 9.95

If you are interested in knowing more about Ramtha's School of Enlightenment, for a free introductory packet call or write to:

Ramtha's School of Enlightenment
PO Box 1210
Yelm, WA 98597
(360) 458-5201 ext. 10
email: audrey@ramtha.com
Website: http://www.ramtha.com